A PEOP
PRAISE

A PEOPLE FOR HIS PRAISE

Renewal and Congregational Life

John Gunstone

HODDER AND STOUGHTON
LONDON SYDNEY AUCKLAND TORONTO

British Library Cataloguing in Publication Data

Gunstone, John
    A people for His praise.——Hodder Christian
paperbacks)
    1. Church of England——Ceremonies and
practices   2. Pentecostalism——Church
of England
    I. Title
264'.03   BX5141

    ISBN 0-340-36098-4

To
Margaret
with much love and gratitude

CONTENTS

INTRODUCTION

The charismatic renewal has been a feature of the Christian world scene for two decades now. Hints that the gifts of the Holy Spirit recorded in Acts were being experienced in the mainline denominations began to spread across the Atlantic in the late 'fifties ("Episcopalians Speak in Tongues" was one headline), and since then Church people in many different countries have been influenced by the movement. It has certainly created problems. In spite of much exhortation by the movement's leaders that spiritual gifts are for the building up of the Church, charismatics have had difficulties in relating their personal experience of the Holy Spirit to the on-going life and worship of their local churches. Clergy have shown signs of unease when charismatics have met to pray in small groups. Friends in the next pew have been puzzled or alarmed by Pentecostal practices. While it is generally acknowledged that some have been helped through the movement—the sick have been healed and the troubled have found peace—there is still much suspicion and misunderstanding around. Some church leaders have given the impression that their dearest wish was that the charismatic renewal would go away!

But charismatics themselves are hopeful. They believe that God is recalling his Church to a fuller realisation of what it means to be the Spirit-filled fellowship which is the body of Jesus Christ, and they look forward to the time when the lessons of the movement will be fully accepted by the denominations to which they belong. There are signs that this is already beginning to happen. Baptism in the Holy Spirit is bringing new life into congregations and new ministries are growing up alongside the traditional ones. Furthermore, if some local churches do not adopt distinctly Pentecostal styles (if they do not become, in Colin Buchanan's phrase, "card-carrying charismatics") nevertheless the movement is helping them to grow in the Spirit.

The forward surge of the charismatic renewal has thrown up a pile of fascinating books. Indeed, there are so many that an author must ask himself if he really has anything fresh to say. The reason I decided to write this one is because there is a gap among the subjects on the pile. There are testimonies by individuals, stories of congregations, instruction manuals on spiritual gifts, and theological works discussing Pentecostalism in the light of the Church's doctrine and liturgy. But there is very little relating the charismatic renewal in a general way to the ordinary congregation.* Only here and there among all these books does the reader find the beginnings of an answer to the nagging question, "That's all very wonderful for you in your church, but what does it mean for me?"

So I have tried to fill that gap—I say "tried" because although the charismatic renewal is twenty years' old, the application of its lessons to the local churches in our denominations is still in its early stages. I have begun with some of the problems that arise between an individual and the congregation when he or she is baptised in the Holy Spirit. Then I have looked at the local church as a creation of the Spirit and gone on to compare it with two distinctive features of the charismatic renewal, the prayer meeting and the prayer group. I have suggested ways in which the movement can enrich the life, leadership, worship, ministry and mission of a congregation. Finally I have discussed the relationship between the institutional and the charismatic dimensions of the Church as it is manifested in the problem of pastoring the renewal movement within the wider Christian fellowship.

I have unashamedly used terms like "baptism in the Holy Spirit" and "charismatics" because the jargon is a handy form of shorthand when writing about this subject. I have employed the word "pastor" to denote an ordained minister in any of the denominations, and "local church" in the sense of a congregation gathered in one place, usually a church building.

I would like to thank the large number of people who have

* The only book I know on this topic is George Martin's *Parish Renewal: A Charismatic Approach* (Word of Life, South Bend, Indiana, 1976), but this is only a limited treatment applicable to a Roman Catholic congregation.

helped me to shape my ideas for this book by telling me their joys and problems, victories and failings, as they sought to follow the Spirit's leading in their own congregations. I am particularly grateful to three friends who allowed me to quote from letters that they wrote—Court Baker, Colin Bond, and Ian Stuchbery.

1

Personal Renewal

At the heart of the charismatic movement is the individual Christian's experience of a Pentecostal baptism in the Holy Spirit. Through this fresh encounter with God's grace, tens of thousands—maybe hundreds of thousands—are being released from personal bondages and equipped with spiritual gifts to minister to others in Christ's name. Although most charismatics would affirm that the experience gives them a deeper appreciation of what John the Baptist meant when he announced that Jesus Christ is "he who baptises with the Holy Spirit" (John 1.33), their personal stories about renewal vary a good deal.

A priest came to me one day and said, "I'd be grateful if you'd pray with me for baptism in the Spirit."

We were sitting by ourselves in my room at a conference.

"But first," he went on, "I'd like to make my confession."

He did this with humility and reverence. I stood up to pronounce the absolution and he knelt on the floor in front of me. After I had said the formula, I placed my hands on his head and prayed that the Lord would anoint him with the Holy Spirit. Almost immediately I felt the priest tremble. Suddenly he lifted up his hands and a guttural, Germanic-sounding language poured from his lips, rising and falling in a beautiful rhythm. A few moments afterwards he stopped, looked up, jumped to his feet and flung his arms round me...

I met a student at a retreat. After I had prayed with him, he sat quietly for a long time. Then he said he believed the Lord was giving him a gift for a ministry of healing. I told him he must ask the Spirit to guide him to someone who would help him embark on that ministry, and he said he would do that. When he got up from his chair, he took something from his pocket and showed me in his hand a small packet of tobacco, an envelope of cigarette papers, and a gadget for rolling cigarettes.

"If I'm to have a healing ministry," he said, "I must be healed of this habit myself."

With those words he dropped the contents of his hand into the wastepaper basket and left. . .

A woman remained in her place at the end of a meeting I had addressed. I talked to her for a while and then she asked me to pray with her. Afterwards she showed no signs of having experienced anything. She thanked me and left the hall. I never saw her again. But three years later she met a priest I knew and, through him, I learned what had happened to her on that night. She had got into her car and driven away. She had not gone many miles before she sensed a comforting warmth spreading through her body. A flood of joy gushed up within her and she began to praise God in a new language. The experience was so unexpected that she involuntarily lifted her hands in the air. The car swerved dangerously. She grabbed the wheel and stopped at the side of the road. For some minutes she sat there, the strange words coming from her lips. Then, looking round, she realised she had pulled up outside a friend's house and she had a sudden impulse to tell her what had happened. As the friend listened, she too felt a warmth within her and, for the first time in *her* life, praised God in tongues as well. . .

There has been much discussion both inside and outside charismatic circles about the nature of baptism in the Spirit. Some understand it as a fresh encounter with God through which the Christian is equipped with power for his ministry and mission; others interpret it as a fuller appropriation by the Christian of all that God gave him when he was initiated into the Church. For the moment we will simply note that the effects of this experience are not the same for everyone. When a Christian is renewed in this way, he does not reach a standard of spiritual maturity which, if it could be measured, would reach the same mark on some mystical scale. What happens depends on a number of things, including the reality of our penitence, the realisation of our needs, the circumstances of our lives, and our willingness to receive God's gifts. The three stories demonstrate this. The priest felt the need for more of God's power in his life because he had come up against spiritual barriers that thwarted his pastoral work. He opened himself to the Lord by confessing his sins and experienced God's love through a charism which assured him he was being re-equipped by the Spirit for his ministry. The student expressed his penitence by discarding a habit which was becoming sinful because of the hold it had over him. He did not receive the gift of tongues but believed he was to exercise another charism which would be tested and discerned by others. The woman felt nothing when prayers were said with her, but shortly afterwards the gift of tongues came as a sign of a new release into God's love. She was able to minister that renewing love to a friend immediately after-wards.

We would expect personal renewals like these to strengthen and enrich the relationships between those who experience them and the congregations of which they are members. In the teaching of the charismatic movement much stress is placed on spiritual gifts as means whereby the Church is built up. Paul's phrase, *pros to sympheron*, "for the common good", "to profit" or "with a view to mutual profit" (1 Corinthians 12.7) is analysed and expounded in talks, articles and books. It is pointed out that a spiritual gift can never be just a personal experience isolated from any practical involvement in the renewing activity of God through Jesus Christ in the Church; it only becomes a charism in the fullest sense when it enables an individual Christian or a group to assist in the mission of the Gospel and the healing of a sick world. When an individual Christian is baptised in the Spirit, then, we look for blessings among the people with whom he lives and worships and serves the Lord.

But it is not always like this. Some charismatics feel a dis-orientation and even an estrangement between themselves and their congregations. Things are not the same as they were before. The Christianity they knew before their baptism in the Spirit seems impoverished when compared with the Christianity into which they are now moving. The activities of the congregation appear mundane and its worship spiritless in contrast with the tide of renewal they experience within the charismatic movement. So they begin to seek fellowship and worship elsewhere. They attend charismatic prayer meetings where they share in a kind of worship that is very different from the Sunday services in their own churches. They join charismatic prayer groups where they experience a bond of fellowship that supports and encourages them more than anything they receive from their pastor and their congregation. The result is not a strengthening of their relationships with the congregation but a weakening of them. Pastors have been baffled because those members of their flock who suddenly seem to grow in faith apparently become dissatisfied with the local church.

I think there are three main reasons for this.

The first lies in the effect of baptism in the Spirit within the individual concerned.

Renewal is never a smooth experience. Those who give the impression that, after baptism in the Spirit, life is filled with the joy of heaven delude themselves and mislead others. It is true that the first weeks after a fresh experience of personal release in the Spirit can be glorious. We are more aware of God's presence than we were before and—like the woman I met at the meeting—find ourselves ministering to others in new and unexpected ways. But then God also begins a process of purification within us. Besides being more aware of his presence, we are also more aware of our weaknesses. We are shown things about ourselves that we did not recognise before: attitudes to others and opinions about ourselves are exposed in all their unloving shallowness and pride. Complacency and self-righteousness are brushed aside as disobedience and selfishness are revealed. Many go through a wilderness of temptations following baptism in the Spirit.

During times like these the charismatic urgently needs the support of other Christians. But often his pastor and the members of the local church to which he belongs are unable to help him. Suspicions and misunderstandings get in the way. The pastor has theological objections to some of the tenets attributed to the charismatic movement, and the members of the congregation are only interested in exorcisms and speaking in tongues. It is not that they are "unspiritual" or "second-class Christians." It is simply that baptism in the Holy Spirit and much that goes with the experience of Pentecostal renewal is totally foreign to most church-goers. Coming mainly from families where church membership has been assumed for generations, they are usually reserved in their attitude towards their religion. Their personal faith in Jesus Christ tends to be taken for granted rather than enthusiastically voiced. They aren't very expectant about God's power; they don't see how Christ's strange prophecy that his disciples would do "greater things than these" could possibly be applied to the Church they know today.

Congregations with strong loyalties in one of the Christian doctrinal traditions usually assume that the charismatic is being unscriptural or holding beliefs that are contrary to the Church's teaching. Many Evangelicals reject the notion of a Pentecostal "second blessing" and have fixed ideas about the meaning and relevance of some of the spiritual gifts listed in the New Testament. Roman Catholics on the whole accept the experience of personal renewal in the Holy Spirit as a sign of spiritual maturity in the individual but feel threatened when charismatics begin to minister in ways that have usually been reserved for the ordained priesthood. More conventional churchgoers are puzzled by and perhaps afraid of the experiential approach to Christianity. To them it doesn't seem right to use expressions such as, "The Lord said to me," or, "The Lord healed me." Claims about the immediacy of God's word and power seem far removed from what most of them remember from Sunday School lessons, confirmation classes, and sermons.

The second reason is to be found among the purely human factors which are involved when an individual in a congregation changes his attitude. In any group, sudden shifts in the ideas and practices of one member can have a disturbing effect on the rest. The congregation to which we belong—perhaps for years—has known us as a certain type of Christian person. They probably noticed changes in us as we grew older but, since these changes were gradual, they learned to accept them. As we move from adolescence to adulthood, or from middle-age to old-age, our friends and acquaintances are generally prepared to make allowances for the differences they detect in us. But when the renewing power of the Holy Spirit suddenly alters our attitude towards our faith, our worship, our expectations of God in his Church, then this is more difficult for them to handle. Baptism in the Spirit can result in quite dramatic changes in people, and those who know them begin to feel that these individuals have become strangers in their midst.

This happened to a woman who was a deacon in a Baptist church. She had been a member of that congregation with her parents since her childhood. Her confession of faith in Jesus

Christ and her baptism at the age of seventeen had been sincere, but about ten years later she experienced a personal renewal in the Holy Spirit which caused considerable changes in her attitudes. As a result she found herself growing out of sympathy with her parents, the pastor, and the other members of the congregation. She discovered that an Anglican vicar in a nearby town had a weekly charismatic prayer meeting and she began to attend it. Eventually, after much heart-searching, she left the Baptist church, was confirmed, and became a communicant member of the Church of England. The upheaval that this caused, especially within her family, can be imagined. But the events are not difficult to interpret. She changed as a person: the changes were too radical for her Baptist parents, pastor and congregation to accept: result —broken relationships.

The third reason why charismatics gather together in meetings and groups outside their congregations is that many local churches are in need of spiritual renewal, and when a member is baptised in the Spirit he becomes acutely aware of this. There is a lack of pastoral effectiveness and evangelistic thrust in the denominations today. The Gospel is not being proclaimed in a way that brings men and women to repentance and faith, and often the spirit of fellowship among Church members is only a pale shadow of what the New Testament teaches about the unity of Christ's disciples in his Spirit. The services, the committee meetings and the organisations that make up so much of the activity of a local church, seem far removed from what the first Christians in Jerusalem enjoyed when they "devoted themselves to the apostles' teaching and fellowship, to the breaking of bread and the prayers" (Acts 2.42).

The quality of the fellowship varies according to the circumstances of each congregation. Paradoxically it is often where the Church is weak numerically that the spirit of fellowship is strong. I have known churches in East London where only a handful of worshippers gather on Sundays and yet where the friendship between the members and their concern for one another have been obvious. But such congregations are usually so occupied with members' support that they are not able to reach out to others. In them the Church becomes a refuge for mutual comfort rather than a dynamic assembly out of which the mission of God's people springs. In larger congregations, on the other hand, members have little opportunity of experiencing a closer fellowship among themselves because there are so many of them. They become used to the congregation as the place where they have casual friendships with a few and nodding acquaintances with many.

Furthermore, the appearances of success are a trap. People enjoy belonging to something that looks as if it is well supported. The line of shiny cars in the road outside the church gate, and the hordes of well-dressed children pouring out of the family service, give the congregation a status in the neighbourhood. It is easy for the pastor to be so caught up in this apparent success that the size of the Sunday morning congregation becomes the centre of his concern. When the departing worshipper shakes him by the hand and says, "A good crowd you've got here again," it sounds like a vote of confidence in his ministry. Similar comments by visiting ecclesiastical superiors have much the same effect! It is not surprising that charismatics find the "successful" congregation the most difficult to relate to. It is in that kind of a congregation that a real *koinonia* in the New Testament sense of "participation in the Spirit," a fellowship among those who are committed to one another in the love of God, is markedly absent. And when you are beginning to experience this fellowship among a group of Christians outside your local church, then the temptation to commit yourself to them instead is very strong.

Unless they are aware of these reasons, charismatics can slip into the dangerous error of regarding themselves as separate from the rest of the congregation. They begin to speak of their local church in terms of "them" and "us". Gratitude for all that they have received in the past from their pastors and congregations can be replaced by a judgemental spirit. Their language becomes uncharitably critical: "Has anything happened at St. Mary's yet?" —"Is the new Methodist minister Spirit-filled?" Unimportant practices associated with Pentecostalism assume a monstrous importance: it becomes a mark of freedom that you should be allowed to speak in tongues during a church service, or lift your hands in the air when you pray. Baptism in the Holy Spirit shrivels into a doctrine to propagate rather than an experience of God's love to share. The temptation creeps in to desert your congregation and make the charismatic prayer meeting your spiritual home.

But in fact few charismatics actually do this. Whatever may have been the divisiveness in Pentecostalism when it emerged at the beginning of this century, when it drew tens of thousands out of the older denominations, there are no signs of this happening as a result of the charismatic renewal. The leaders insist in their teaching and writing that the Holy Spirit renews the individual Christian for his ministry in the Church (and "the Church" is always interpreted as meaning the congregation to which one already belongs). The vast majority of those who are baptised in the Spirit remain loyal to their local churches in spite of misunderstandings and tensions. Indeed, they sense a fundamental unity between what they have inherited in their traditions and their increasing awareness of God's presence and power in their lives. No matter how lifeless their own congregation might seem to be, they realise that what that congregation represents is very much related to their personal experience. Charismatic Anglicans, for example, find in the words of the *Prayer Book* and the new alternative services much that expresses what the Spirit wants them to say when they confess, intercede and praise God. The scripture readings in the services, the psalms, the canticles, the prayers and the hymns come alive in a new way. So do the sacraments and gifts of the Spirit enshrined in Anglican offices and ministries. For those in other denominations the effect is similar. The Church and the renewal belong together.

In fact, it is gravely misleading to discuss the charismatic movement as if it was something separate from the Church. To speak in this way implies that the Church is nothing but an institution lacking in real spiritual life and that the charismatic movement is like a divine doctor injecting new vigour into her. Nothing could be further from the truth. Strictly speaking, there is no such thing as "the institutional Church". There is only one Church which has various dimensions that are intimately related to one another—the charismatic dimension which sees the Church as the creation of the Holy Spirit; the sacramental dimension which sees the Church as an outward and visible sign of Jesus Christ's presence among his people; the social dimension which sees the Church as a human society within the total society of the nation or the world; and the institutional dimension which sees the Church as an organisation which enables its members to relate to one another and to other institutions. From one dimension,

then, the Church *is* the charismatic movement. We do not belong
to the Church on the one hand and the charismatic movement on
the other. When we are personally renewed, we come to realise
with greater thankfulness and hope that the body of Christ is a
fellowship in him through the Spirit, and therefore the charismatic dimension of the Church grows in significance for us.

When we speak of the lessons of the charismatic movement,
therefore, we are referring to what the Church can learn from
what she already is in Christ Jesus. We are not suggesting that
people outside the Christian fold are saying something to those
inside. God is now at work among all his people, as he always has
been, revealing himself to them and encouraging them to fulfil the
purpose he has for them. Sometimes he reveals that purpose
through individuals, sometimes through groups. The history of
the Church is the history of a movement among people who are
guided and strengthened for their pilgrimage by smaller movements among their own members. Thus is the Gospel renewed as a
living reality among them at different stages on that pilgrimage.
Through the charismatic movement, the Lord is telling his people
to have greater faith in what they are and in what they can become
through the death and resurrection of Jesus Christ and the Pentecostal outpouring of his Spirit. He is telling them to be fully aware
of what it means to be baptised and to be fully open to Jesus
Christ, having met him personally in their lives. He is telling them
to discover afresh each day his identity as Father, Son and Holy
Spirit, and to accept the authority of their Christian discipleship.
If the charismatic movement does nothing more than to uni-
versalise the release of the Spirit, it will have taken the Church
forward in another step on her pilgrimage.

But I anticipate. This discussion should be reserved until later in
the book. The point I am making is that when we can be objective
about our experience of baptism in the Spirit—and we are more
likely to be objective when we have come through the early
difficulties and testings than when we are in the midst of
them—then we shall realise that our personal renewal has everything to do with our local church as it is and not as we hope it
might be one day. For the members of the congregation are men
and women in whom God is at work now, by the power of the
same Spirit. The Lord's blessing is for them as well. As C. S. Lewis
wrote in a little pamphlet called *The Weight of Glory* years ago,

"It is a serious thing to live in a society of possible gods and goddesses, to remember that the dullest and most uninteresting person you talk to may one day be a creature which, if you saw now, you would be strongly tempted to worship, or else a horror. All day long we are, in some degree, helping each other to one or other of these destinies."

2

The Local Church

Let us imagine that we are looking in at a TV programme broadcast from a parish church one Sunday morning. An ingenious producer has sent a camera team aloft in a helicopter to show viewers the members of the congregation as they leave their homes to come to church. Some walk along the streets, others get out of cars parked in the road beside the churchyard. Their shadows thrown by the bright sunlight are like the figures in a Lowry painting. We see one shadow—that of the parish priest in his cassock—flit along the pathway leading from the vicarage to the vestry door.

Many congregations are formed by the coming together of Christians within a geographical area. Parish boundaries originated in this way in early medieval Europe: lines drawn round a neighbourhood in which the inhabitants gathered for worship in a particular building. The old ceremony of "beating the bounds" was the way a parish claimed its area each year. But in modern times the pattern has become more complicated because geographical boundaries have very little relevance in contemporary society. Different denominations draw their congregations from overlapping catchment areas, and an increasing number of Christians come together for worship within other social groupings—the staff and students of a college or a university, the medical staff and patients of a hospital, members of the armed forces in their chapels, and a group of friends in one another's homes. But however and wherever Christians gather, the result is the same. They are, by their coming together, a manifestation of the Church. For wherever two or three are assembled in Christ's name, there is his body—in an ancient parish church, in a modern worship centre, in the chapel of an institution, in the living room of a private house.

What we see on the TV screen, then, is an illustrated definition of the meaning of the word "Church". The Hebrew, *quhal*, usually translated *ecclesia* in the Greek Bible, was used in the Old Testament to describe an assembling of the Israelites or the mustering of men of military age for war. In the Book of Deuteronomy it is used to describe the gathering of the people at Horeb to hear the reading of the Law. With this connotation—of people coming from all quarters to form an assembly—the word is employed in the New Testament as a title for the children of the new covenant responding to the summons of the Father through his Son in the power of the Holy Spirit. In this way a local congregation is a creation of the Spirit because his is the impulse that brings the people together: they have heard the voice of him who is calling them "out of darkness into his marvellous light" (I Peter 2.9.)

A sociologist would tell us that the motives which prompt individuals and families to go to church are varied and complex. People are stirred by ideas, emotions and habits, by social custom, by a search for personal identity, by a need for support and approval from others, and by vague desires to find a purpose for living. From the standpoint of his own discipline, no doubt the sociologist's judgement is valid. His concern is with people's observable behaviour. But a Christian cannot interpret their coming together solely in behaviourist terms. Because of his faith in a God who speaks and acts, he sees the coming together of a congregation as the work of the Holy Spirit. For him these men and women are responding—in ways that differ with each individual—to the call of God. The motives attributed to them by the sociologist may well be elements in their response, but they do not provide the ultimate explanation for the existence of a local church. God moves in many mysterious ways—including those human promptings and aspirations which the sociologist can detect.

Since it is the Lord who brings his people together, we must beware of judging a particular congregation—or a group within it—simply because its way of responding to God's call in worship and in other activities does not always coincide precisely with ours. It does not mean that churchgoers are not open to the Holy Spirit because we cannot attach the charismatic label to them. Diversities between congregations and within them can be caused by sin, but not always. Differences can also reflect the richness of the Church and the variety of human life. God calls to himself men and women from an enormous variety of social, cultural and temperamental backgrounds. Provided individuals and groups, congregations and denominations, are seeking through the Holy Spirit to glorify Jesus Christ as Lord and Saviour, with a growing understanding of and love for other Christians, then their diversity is as beautiful as the variety of flowers within a garden. Dr Russell Spittler, a minister of the Assemblies of God, once asked the members of his denomination at a conference: "How is it that God was able to get along for nearly nineteen hundred years without the Pentecostal Churches?" Charismatics who feel impatient with the traditionalism of their own denominations might well ask themselves the same question!

Differences between Christians are only sinful when they separate us from God. We may not always understand why others' response to God takes the form it does, we may not agree with the way in which they want to respond, and we may sometimes feel justified in disassociating ourselves from it; but we should never, on our own judgement alone, assume that members of a congregation are in total disobedience to God. Such a judgement can only emerge out of a long and careful process of discernment by the whole Church of which we are members. "There are many parts, yet one body. The eye cannot say to the hand, 'I have no need of you', nor again the head to the feet, 'I have no need of you'" (I Corinthians 12.21.) It is with the apostle's teaching on variety within the body of Christ that a charismatic should look at the congregation of which he is a member. As the Lord becomes more real to us through his Spirit, so does our unity with one another in him.

We return to our imaginary TV programme. The cameras have now gone into the church. The sung eucharist has just begun. After giving us a general view of the congregation, the cameras zoom in, throwing close-ups of certain individuals onto the screen. We will assume that we know something about these individuals personally.

First we see the parish priest whom we had noticed coming across the path from the vicarage. He stands at the altar, vested, waiting for the hymn to finish so that he can chant the collect. He has been vicar of this parish for five years and he is wondering if he should write to the bishop asking for a move elsewhere. He finds the pastoral work in this place unrewarding. The people do not respond to the plans he puts before them to promote the Church's mission in that neighbourhood, and he is beginning to think that they should have someone else to lead them.

The picture on the screen slides as the camera moves to pick out the organist, swaying from side to side as his hands and feet touch the keys and the pedals. He plays well, encouraging the sluggish singing with bold, brief chords. He loves the traditional music of the Church and is never happier than when he is seated at the organ. He is less happy when he tries to teach the choir at the weekly practice. He lacks that subtle combination of devotion, authority and humour that is necessary in a good choirmaster.

In the front pew is an elderly lady. Her fresh hair-do and new coat do not conceal the loneliness and sadness that shadow her. When her husband died two years ago, she was much helped by the kindness of the parish priest and began attending the church on the Sunday after the funeral. Perhaps she had a ghost of a notion that in church she would somehow be closer to her departed spouse. Certainly she derives much support from the services. But she would be embarrassed if she was asked if she loved Jesus Christ. She would say she wasn't "too religious". Yet she has a sympathy for strangers in the congregation, especially if she senses they are troubled. She talks to them after the service and sometimes invites them to her home for coffee.

Behind her stand a married couple. Their daughter, aged nine, sits between them (their son, aged four, is in the Sunday School organised in the vestry during the service: during moments of silence in church the children's voices can just be heard). The husband had a conversion experience when he attended an Evangelical church in his student days. He has a gnawing sense of frustration because he isn't being used to bring others to a living faith in Jesus Christ. This is partly because he doesn't get on too well with the parish priest, and partly because his wife is, by his standards, far too liberal in her theological outlook (she says that the goodness of God can be seen in all people whatever their religion—or none). Their daughter enjoys the hymns but is bored by everything else. What she likes most about the service is that it is one hour in the week when she has her parents all to herself.

The camera flits over the pews to pick out three boys, aged about fifteen, standing with their hymnbooks open and their mouths shut. They are gazing towards the east window with vacant expressions on their faces. They are the survivors of last year's confirmation class. For them the service is neither interesting nor tedious, just familiar. It enables them to escape from the depressing Sunday morning atmosphere of their homes and to meet their girl-friends (in a pew on the other side of the church) afterwards. We know that one of them has a leadership role in the lives of the other two. When he says on Saturdays, "See you at church tomorrow," they feel a compulsion to go with him. He is beginning to read paperbacks about the Christian faith and to dip into the Bible.

Beyond the boys are an older couple who have attended this church since they bought a house in the district as newly-weds thirty-five years ago. In their youth they were brought up in an Anglo-Catholic parish where they were taught that "mass on Sundays and Holy Days" was the basis for Christian living, and their involvement with the congregation has been rooted in this precept. They have not welcomed the changes they have witnessed in the church's worship during recent years and the experience has left them with a waspish attitude towards the vicar and the other members. In their eyes today's clergy and communicants fall far below the standards of firm doctrine and iron discipline that they once admired. In spite of this, they are respected as "the old faithfuls". The husband is elected as treasurer year after year because he fulfils that office efficiently and conscientiously: on Sunday evenings he collects the money from the vestry safe, counts it with meticulous care, banks it on Monday mornings, and keeps the books with such accuracy that the auditor feels it is hardly worthwhile looking at them. The wife acts as secretary to the weekly women's meeting with the same care: she pushes the committee into fixing the programme for the meetings six months in advance and visits sick members in a slightly off-hand but well-meant way.

The camera moves on up the aisle...

How does the New Testament teaching on the gifts of the Spirit relate to a congregation like this? Uncritical reliance on the teaching of some of the classical Pentecostal Churches in answering this question can be misleading. With their view of scripture Pentecostals have tended to absolutise the charisms described in Acts and the Pauline epistles in a way that has limited the interpretation of these spiritual gifts and excluded others. For example, Pentecostals have said that each local church should manifest within its fellowship the gifts listed in I Corinthians 12 or the ministries in Ephesians 4, implying that if these gifts and ministries were not evident something was missing from that local church's life. Charismatics within the established denominations, experiencing for the first time tongues, interpretations, prophecies and healings, have been troubled by this view and wondered if their own congregations were devoid of spiritual gifts because these charisms were unknown among them.

A more accurate interpretation of the New Testament passages gives a more reassuring answer. The Greek word *charisma* ("free gift of grace") is not used in a technical, theological sense; it is employed to describe almost any act of God which is freely given and entirely unmerited. The word is used for acts as diverse as a divinely given ability to prophesy and a miraculous release from prison. Indeed, the supreme gift of all, "eternal life in Christ Jesus our Lord", is the *charisma* of God (Romans 6.23). Perhaps what attracted Paul's attention to this word—he uses it more than any other New Testament writer—is that etymologically it reflected the free grace (*charis*) of God, a concept that is the keystone to so much of his teaching. It was, therefore, a fairly straightforward development for the apostle to use this word when he wanted to refer to the manner in which God empowered and equipped individuals by the Holy Spirit to enable them to fulfil his purposes in the body of Christ. By using it in this way in such passages as Romans 12.6, I Corinthians 1.7 and 12.4,9,28,30,31, Paul gave *charisma* a more specific meaning—gifts of the Spirit that equipped the Christian for particular kinds of ministries. The word also has this meaning in I Peter 4.10.

According to the New Testament, then, spiritual gifts are unlimited in number and range. The concretisation of divine grace (to coin the ugly phrase of contemporary theologians) manifests itself in a wide variety of activities, not only in outstanding powers of a supernatural kind but also in very down-to-earth abilities. The lists of charisms in the epistles are not exhaustive but they include a wide selection: through the gift of God's grace Christians are enabled to speak words of divine wisdom, to put the deepest knowledge into language which others can understand, to receive extraordinary faith, to heal, to perform miracles, to prophesy, to discern spirits, to speak in tongues and to interpret tongues (I Corinthians 12.6–8); to minister as apostles, prophets, teachers, miracle-workers, healers, helpers, guides to others and glossolists (I Corinthians 12.28); to be prophets, administrators, teachers, encouragers of others, generous givers, leaders in the congregation, and aids for those in need (Romans 12.6–8.) Marriage and celibacy require gifts of God's grace. So does the acceptance of martyrdom in the name of Christ.

The charismatic movement is re-educating us in the Church's need for those spiritual gifts because we have tended to think of them as belonging only to the early days of Christianity. We used to believe that charisms such as prophecy, tongues, interpretations and healings ceased long ago. It did not seem reasonable to expect the Lord to give his Church prophets in these days of widespread teaching and mass communications, and it did not seem likely that miraculous healings would take place after prayer when so many near-miracles were being performed every day through the advance of medical science. Now we are realising afresh that such gifts are still available to the Church, if we have the faith to minister to others in the confidence that God will act with power. For this we have much to thank the classical Pentecostal Churches. The Lord has used them in recent years to recall the rest of his Church to all that he offers his people by grace. Nevertheless, I do not mean to be unkind when I say that the teaching of some Pentecostals on spiritual gifts can be narrowing as well as liberating. It can, if accepted uncritically, blind us to the reality of those less spectacular and more humble charisms which are to be found in the kind of congregation I have just described, and which also build up the Church and forward its mission.

In 1974 a group of Roman Catholic theologians involved in the charismatic renewal in their own Church met at Malines and drew up a statement on *Theological and Pastoral Orientations on the Catholic Charismatic Renewal*. In it there is an illustration which clarifies the teaching of the charismatic movement about spiritual gifts. It goes like this. Let us assume that we can catalogue all the gifts of the Spirit under the letters of the alphabet A to Z (the charisms cannot, of course, be limited in this way, but for the purposes of this illustration we will assume they can). In this catalogue, charisms A to P are those spiritual gifts which are in evidence in most congregations—generosity in giving money to the Church and other charitable causes, acts of kindness to those in need, teaching in Sunday School, offering hospitality of all kinds, keeping the accounts, singing in the choir. The charisms Q to Z, however, are those spiritual gifts which have been neglected and which are being rediscovered through the Pentecostal Churches—prophecy, tongues, interpretations, healings, and so on. What the charismatic movement has to say to most congregations, therefore, is, "Are you aware that these Q to Z charisms may also be necessary to strengthen your corporate life in Christ and to minister to others in his name?"

We switch off our imaginary TV programme, close our eyes, and think of the people who appeared on the screen. We can thank God for them—as Paul thanked him for all the spiritual gifts he recognised in the congregations he knew. But we can also dream of a time when those gifts will result in a more effective life and a more powerful mission. We have discerned some of the A to P charisms in those people in church; we picture what might happen if the Q to Z charisms were evident as well. The priest would realise more confidently the gift of the Holy Spirit that was his to act as pastor of the local church. He would be less concerned about persuading the congregation to accept his ideas for mission. Instead he would call them to pray with him to seek God's word through prophecy concerning their mission in their neighbourhood. The organist would offer his musical talents to God's glory rather than pursue them for his own satisfaction. He would come to regard the choir, not as a musical instrument, but as a group that shared with him a ministry of enabling the congregation to be joyful before the Lord. The widow would find that she had more than natural sympathy to offer the lonely. She would be used by the Spirit to bring a transfiguring comfort into their lives, turning their sorrow into joy. The married couple would realise a deeper unity with one another in Christ. They would accept their differences in temperament and outlook as the Lord's way of equipping them for mission, demonstrating through their family life with their children that the proclamation of the Gospel and its working out in practical service for others is not restricted to one man's or one woman's expression of it. The boy would grow into a spirituality far maturer than his years. He would be used among his friends as one who took the initiative of a leader in the name of Jesus Christ. The elderly couple would be released from their bitterness and given a love for others that made them more than respected elders. Their experience of life in the Church would be used in a gift of wisdom for the ministry of the congregation. . .

Are these only dreams? Charismatics sometimes come to think so after dreaming what might have been for a very long time! It is not surprising that they sometimes give up hope when they have worshipped in a particular church for years and witnessed no sign of renewal in its pastor and members. Should they transfer their allegiance to another congregation? It isn't an easy question to answer. Much depends on their personal circumstances. When someone comes to me with this problem, I usually try to explore his or her feelings of responsibility in the matter. The Lord does occasionally lead us out of one local church and into another. A father of a young family might feel that it is right to take his wife and children to somewhere where the worship and the fellowship is more open to the Holy Spirit. But I think most charismatics are being told by the Lord to stay where they are. "I have revealed more of my love for you," he seems to say. "Now show me more of your love in your loyalty to these unresponsive children of mine!"

So charismatics are left with their dreams. But the Lord has a way of preparing his servants for his work through dreams. They can be prophetic visions for those who are anointed by the Spirit. And the long wait can be wonderfully rewarded. An elderly Anglican prayed for many years that spiritual renewal would come to her parish church. Even when it was threatened with closure, she went on praying. And she saw her dream become a reality. She was a member of what was once a dwindling congregation in a downtown part of Houston, Texas, in the Church of the Redeemer. . .

3

The Prayer Meeting

The prayer meeting and the prayer group are two wellknown expressions of the charismatic renewal. For charismatics these gatherings are precious links with the movement that has powerfully influenced their spiritual growth, but for others in the congregation they are rather puzzling, even threatening, gatherings. What are they for? it is asked. What happens at them? What is there in them for us? We must, therefore, examine the nature and significance of these meetings. In this chapter we shall discuss the prayer meeting. The prayer group will occupy our attention in the chapter after that.

A charismatic prayer meeting takes place when Christians come together with the expectation that God will speak and act through them, especially through the Pentecostal gifts. The number attending may vary from tens to tens of thousands. A prayer meeting arranged in a local church for members of the congregation may only consist of thirty or forty. The prayer meeting that ended the 1977 national conference on charismatic renewal in the United States in Kansas City totalled nearly fifty thousand. Most of the meetings I have attended have numbered between a hundred and a thousand. Historically the charismatic prayer meeting is a descendant of the huge gatherings drawn together by the evangelistic ministry of teams like Moody and Sankey, and Torrey and Alexander, in the latter half of the nineteenth century. The style of these meetings was adapted by the Pentecostal Churches at the beginning of this century. Within the charismatic renewal these meetings are rather more restrained than their classical Pentecostal counterpart. Nevertheless, on the average churchgoer belonging to one of the traditional denominations, attending a charismatic prayer meeting for the first time, it can inflict something not far removed from a religio-cultural shock!

The keynote of these meetings is praise. Under the impulse of the Holy Spirit Christians are being given a fresh release into praise. Because corporate acts of praise in most church services are controlled by the formality of their liturgies, many church-goers have never experienced praise as an abandonment to the spirit of joy that can sweep through a Christian congregation as it responds to the love of God. They have known praise only as a fixed expression (at its most extreme form in the unrevised rite of the Roman Catholic Church: *Alleluias* could be doubled—said twice—during Eastertide!) The only feeling they have experienced in praise was when they had a momentary thrill at the climax of a hymn such as *Praise to the Lord, the Almighty, the King of creation*. For them the spontaneous praises at a charismatic prayer meeting are quite novel. They have never known what it means to be part of an assembly that praises for ten minutes or a quarter-of-an-hour by moving easily from choruses to psalms, from shouts of acclamation to minutes filled with the silence of adoration. They begin to discover for the first time that praise is not just a form of words used in church services but a pivotal expression of their faith.

Praise gives voice to our fundamental belief that we are Christians because God has an ultimate purpose for us with himself in heaven. Our creation and redemption are for his glory. In praise we declare our love of God in union with Jesus Christ, whose whole mission, from his conception in the womb of the Virgin Mary to his ascension into heaven, was one glorious shout of praise to the Father. On the eve of the crucifixion the Christ of the fourth gospel could praise his Father because he knew that his victory was all but accomplished: "I glorified thee on earth, having accomplished the work which thou gavest me to do; and now, Father, glorify thou me in thy own presence with the glory which I had with thee before the world was made." And he could pray that his disciples would share in that glory: "Father, I desire that they also, whom thou hast given me, may be with me where I am, to behold my glory which thou hast given me in thy love for me before the foundation of the world" (John 17. 4–5, 24). Because the Holy Spirit unites us with the risen Christ, his praise is our praise, too. To be members of his body is to be one with that heavenly host who sing, "Holy, holy, holy, is the Lord God Almighty, who was and is and is to come!" (Revelation 4. 8).

This is one of the correctives that the charismatic renewal is applying to our concept of what it means to be the Church of God. In recent years there has been much stress on the Church as the company of those who are called by God to serve him in serving others in the world. I Peter 2.9 is the scriptural passage frequently quoted to support this teaching. We are told that we are a people chosen by God to share in the royal and priestly ministry of Jesus Christ. The verse is used as a text for numerous sermons on this theme. It is, of course, an important aspect of the Church's mission—as we shall recognise in a later chapter. But it is not the whole of it—nor the most important part of it. The second half of that verse from I Peter (which isn't often quoted with the first half in sermons!) makes that plain. It explains *why* we are a people chosen by God. The translation in the Jerusalem Bible is one of the clearest: "You are a chosen race, a royal priesthood, a consecrated nation, a people set apart *to sing the praises of God*" (my italics). In other words, everything else we are called to do—proclaiming the Gospel of the Kingdom, loving the brotherhood, ministering to one another and to others—is to express our praise of God. As Augustine of Hippo once deliciously put it, a Christian is to be "an *Alleluia* from head to foot, from top to toe".

My first visit to a charismatic prayer meeting was an embarrassing experience. I had never been to anything like it before. Speakers referred to the Lord as if they were on intimate terms with him. Hands were lifted in the air. One chorus followed another in an interminable procession, and participants appeared to be carried away by praise in a manner that was totally foreign to what I had been used to in the Church of England. Worst of all, I felt miserably conspicuous because of my inability to join in. I must have looked like one of those wallflowers at a party who refuse to get involved in the fun.

This embarrassment gradually thawed as the Holy Spirit began dealing with my self-consciousness and my prejudices. I found a new liberation in lifting my hands and holding my head up during prayer. Things that I had said and done only formally in church I now began to say and do more freely. I ventured a few spontaneous prayers at meetings, then a prayer in tongues, then (more venturesome still!) an interpretation of tongues. But it wasn't easy. I seemed to live a double life as far as worship was concerned—behaving in one way during prayer meetings and another way during church services. I wondered what those who went to church services would think if they could see me at prayer meetings!

That was years ago. Now I am as much at home in a lively charismatic prayer meeting as I am in a solemn cathedral even-song (and, may I add, I usually feel as free in the Spirit to worship God in one as in the other: I discovered this when I once attended both kinds of gatherings in one day in London). But memories of that personal tension have left me with much sympathy for those Christians who feel like liturgical schizoids when they go to a charismatic prayer meeting one weekday evening and to a church service the following Sunday morning. No wonder some regard the charismatic prayer meeting as a protest against the over-formality of church services!

We shall, I hope, be able to see later that the division between the two is not as great as appears at first sight. In the meantime, when we examine the contents of charismatic prayer meetings, we discover that, in spite of the spontaneity and variety that these gatherings contain, they nearly always include four basic elements.

(1) *An Introduction.* This element helps those who are coming together to prepare to hear God's Word and to respond to him. It might include a warming-up session of chorus-singing. It will also include the notices about who's who among the participants and the explanations to help those present to understand what is happening and to join in. Under this heading we can add preliminary acts of praise to God at the beginning of the meeting and petitions for personal cleansing and inspiration.

(2) *The Ministry of the Word of God.* This element is focussed on the reading of the scriptures and the teaching given by the main speaker. But a characteristic of the charismatic prayer meeting is that participants expect God to speak in other ways, too—a gift of prophecy that allows the voice of the Lord to be heard with dramatic relevance to those present, a spontaneous testimony by an individual, a sentence or two from the Bible or from some other source inspired at the very moment when the words uttered speak directly to the meeting. Usually a definite theme emerges through what is said and sung, and we frequently come away with the impression that God has spoken to us individually or corporately

in a particular way that evening. Indeed, the validity of this impression (how it bears on our lives during the following days and helps us through various personal circumstances) is one of the tests for discerning the guidance of the Holy Spirit at the meeting.

(3) *The Response by the People.* For most of those present this element is represented by the prayers for forgiveness, guidance and strength, and by the acts of thanksgiving and praise that are made, usually in the latter part of the meeting. But it can also include the response made by the individual who goes forward for counselling, or for prayers for healing, or for baptism in the Holy Spirit. Sometimes the response will include singing and dancing in the Spirit as well as other demonstrations of joy in the Lord. The prayer meeting is flexible enough to permit responses of all kinds from individuals, groups, and the whole assembly itself, provided they are directed towards God in the spirit of love for him and for those present. Prayer meetings among Pentecostals usually end with an altar call, an invitation to individuals to come to the front of the gathering to commit themselves to Jesus Christ or to make special requests for ministry. Among charismatics this is not so common. Ministry to those requiring it is generally given after the meeting privately in small groups.

(4) *The Dismissal.* As in all services and meetings, the ending of the proceedings is at least as important as the introduction—if not more so, for the way in which people are dismissed rounds off the impression they have received of the prayer meeting as a whole. A few words summing up what has been learned, an appropriate chorus or hymn, and a blessing help people to remember that the grace of God continues with them as they go home. In the *Dismissal* it is often possible to point out the link between the prayer meeting and their own local churches—that God will be present at the service the following Sunday, speaking to them and equipping them with his spiritual gifts.

Although a charismatic prayer meeting is extremely flexible, and to the casual observer seems to happen freely and in an unplanned way, it does in fact require a good deal of preparation by a group of people who accept the responsibility for organising it as part of their Christian ministry. Although we cannot limit the effectiveness of the Spirit to the efficiency of our preparations, experience shows that the success of a big prayer meeting depends to a considerable extent on the way this core group prepares for it. This includes not only their arrangements for the meeting and their teamwork while it is taking place, but also their follow-up with individuals afterwards. Without them the meeting would collapse as a non-event.

In the summer of 1976 I was invited to address a prayer meeting in Birmingham. I arrived at the Central Hall in Corporation Street about three-quarters of an hour before it was timed to begin, and I was led into a room where about twenty people sat in a circle praying. The leader, an Anglican priest, briefly welcomed me and then the group went on with their prayers, involving me in them. Individuals slipped in and out to attend to various matters—the ushers left when someone said that people were beginning to arrive at the main door of the hall, and a musician was called out to trace a fault in a piece of amplification equipment—but nothing was allowed to disturb the atmosphere of relaxed devotion and waiting on God. We left the room and I took my place on the stage with the leader just as the warm-up was drawing to a close.

Prayer meetings usually have a pianist and/or a music group and sometimes a choir. (Organists are not used very much: is this a sign of reaction against the traditional church service?) Their ministry is to assist the meeting in song—not only the set pieces such as hymns, choruses and solo items, but also in accompanying various spontaneous items. Some groups can accompany singing in the Spirit in a beautiful way. Much depends on their attitude towards the meeting. As long as they continue to offer their skills as gifts in the Lord's service, the meeting will be blessed by their presence. But woe to that meeting if the music group regards it as an audience before which they can demonstrate their talents! The repertoire of choruses and hymns tends to change each year. While song-books are useful (for example, Jeanne Harper and Betty Pulkingham's *Sounds of Living Water* and *Fresh Sounds*) most core groups find it worthwhile making their own collection.

Besides the musicians and choir there are also counsellors and ushers, mingling among the people, manning the bookstall, giving out chorus-sheets and hymnbooks, taking the collection, and listening to and praying with those who ask for ministry during or after the proceedings. If there are to be ministries of healing and deliverance, it is wise to have a doctor and a nurse available. One speaker who is much used in the ministry of deliverance always has members of the medical profession in his team of assistants. The bookstall is a valuable asset. Books, magazines and cassettes on the charismatic renewal are not always easy to obtain when potential customers do not live near a Christian bookshop, and good books are necessary for the on-going teaching about the renewal. Recommendations about books are often included in the notices or talks.

Then there are those who take a special part in the meeting—giving out the notices, reading the scriptures, guiding the intercessions. Their contributions have to be prepared as well: muddled notices, inaudible readings and mumbled prayers are dishonouring to the Lord and discouraging for those who listen to them.

The chief responsibility for the meeting rests on the shoulders of the one who presides over it. He has the vital ministry of weaving together what has been prepared and rehearsed with what is offered spontaneously. He needs to be relaxed to enable others to relax as well, but he has to keep control over the proceedings so that each contribution adds to a forward-moving, coherent and uplifting act of worship. With greater freedom in the Spirit there must also be a greater discipline (a principle that can be applied to other forms of Christian activity!) In a large gathering there will nearly always be someone who is insensitive to the movement of the Spirit and who will, perhaps unconsciously, use the occasion for self-display. Such individuals have to be dealt with gently but firmly. Also, when a large number of people come together not quite sure what is going to happen, a sense of apprehension can spread among them (notice how even the most trivial remarks at the beginning of a charismatic prayer meeting produce spasms of nervous giggling); they have to be reassured by the knowledge that the leader is capable of dealing with anything disturbing or unexpected that might happen.

A charismatic meeting of about three hundred people in the Westminster Cathedral Centre in London opened one day with an hour's prayer, praise, singing in the Spirit, and a few testimonies and scripture readings. Then the Roman Catholic priest who was leading suggested that we should spend some time in silence listening to God in our hearts.

The silence had only lasted a minute or two when a woman spoke.

"Father, I believe the Lord wants to say something."

The priest looked at her.

"Are you sure it is the Lord?" he asked sternly.

"Yes, father."

"Won't you wait until later?"

"I believe I should speak now, father."

"Very well, then go ahead."

The woman spoke a word of wisdom. I do not remember its substance, but it had an authority that seemed to come from beyond her, and it was relevant for some who were present for they thanked the Lord for it. For me, however, it was a memorable illustration of the way in which order should be preserved when spiritual gifts are exercised in a meeting. The fact that the priest challenged the woman about her inspiration caused her to test for herself whether or not what she had to say was of God.

Leadership is one of the gifts of the Holy Spirit to the Church for building up of the people of God and for their encouragement. One of the Greek words used to describe this charism is *kybernēsis* ("administrator" in the RSV of I Corinthians 12.28). *Kybernēsis* is from the language of sailors: it means the one who steers a ship. This is an evocative analogy. The leader of the prayer meeting is the man at the helm. The gathering is driven along by the wind of the Spirit, but unless the leader's hand is firmly on the tiller, there is every danger that the ship's course may be deflected by the cross-currents of human emotions and ambitions that move not very far below the surface of the sea over which she sails.

When I have led charismatic prayer meetings I have found it helpful to keep in mind the four basic elements I have just listed and to catalogue mentally each spontaneous contribution as it is given. This assists me to discern the nature of each contribution and to fit it in with everything else in the meeting. Sometimes I have had to tell a participant that he should postpone his contribution until later. For example, it may be that immediately after an address by the visiting speaker intercessions are made by one or two at the meeting, asking for the grace of God to enable them to fulfil the teaching he has revealed. These intercessions blend together to form the beginning of a *Response by the People* when suddenly an individual stands up to give a prophecy which is apparently unconnected with what the meeting has been hearing. Time is needed to test the prophecy (a possible further contribution to the *Ministry of the Word*), but to do so at that moment would divert the meeting from its spontaneous *Response*. In these circumstances I would probably suggest that we keep the terms of the prophecy in our minds until the intercessions are over and then I will lead the meeting's thoughts back to it. Again, there may be occasions when it is necessary to check a meeting's *Response* and bring it back to the *Ministry of the Word*. Singing can get out of hand. Chorus after chorus can follow one another so that the meeting's *Response* degenerates into a trip through the top twenty among the latest choruses without much thought of what the words mean. Singing of this kind is no more an expression of praise than the songs of the church men's club on their way back from their annual outing in a coach! When this happens, I call a halt and redirect the meeting's attention to the content of the *Ministry of the Word*, perhaps by reading again a few verses from the scriptures or going over some of the points made by the speaker. This helps the meeting to re-examine the form its *Response* is taking.

On the desk in front of me I usually have a piece of paper divided into four sections. One section is allocated to each of the elements I have just described. In each section I note down what has been prepared—details of what I am to announce in (1), scripture references in (2), the numbers of the choruses in the sections where they may be most appropriately sung, and so on. But I leave room in the sections to jot down a few words about the spontaneous contributions if and when they occur. This is especially useful for making notes about prophecies and interpretations as they are given, details about healings described in personal testimonies, and the number of a chorus that I suddenly think of. The following illustrates the kind of things that can be noted in the four sections:

(1) *Introduction*
Prepared ——Welcome.
          Notices (name of speaker, theme of meeting, date of next meeting).
          Explanations of arrangements (opportunities for personal ministry after the meeting).

Introductory prayers.
Hymns and choruses.

Spontaneous——Requests for choruses.
Additional notices from individuals present.

(2) *Ministry of the Word of God*

Prepared ——Scripture reading(s).
Address.
Invited testimonies from individuals.
Further readings, dramatic presentations, mime, dance, songs, visual aids, &c.

Spontaneous——More readings by individuals (usually a verse of scripture).
Testimonies.
Prophecies, tongues and interpretations, words of wisdom, descriptions of inspired pictures or visions.

(3) *Response by the People*

Prepared ——Hymns, canticles, psalms and choruses.
Solo items.
Invitations to pre-arranged activities (counselling, involvement in projects).

Spontaneous——Choruses and songs.
Singing in the Spirit.
Periods of silence.
Prayers and requests for prayer.

(4) *Dismissal*

Prepared ——Final exhortations.
Choruses.

Spontaneous——Words of encouragement.
Final songs and prayers.

With this outline in front of me, I find it easier to comment on events as they take place and to provide a unifying thread of explanation during the meeting. Bearing in mind that newcomers may be unfamiliar with the Pentecostal charisms of prayer, this commentary is necessary for them even if the rest of the meeting is capable of responding to God without too much direction. For instance, during the first few minutes' introductory prayer someone may speak in tongues. If I know that there are newcomers present, I say something like this when the glossolist has finished: "That was a gift of tongues. We will ask the Lord to anoint someone here to give the interpretation." After the interpretation has been given, I then add, "We will think about those words for a few moments and test to see whether the Lord is saying anything to us through them." If no interpretation is given, I suggest we go on to the next item believing that God will speak to us in another way. A commentary like this helps people who are not used to charismatic prayer meetings to overcome their feeling of alienation caused by unfamiliarity. They sense an order and purpose behind what they see and hear, and this encourages them to participate in the proceedings rather than to remain a spectator.

Common mistakes made by leaders are:

> allowing the chorus singing to go on for too long;
> forgetting to let people stand after sitting through a long address;
> allowing individuals to dominate the proceedings with their own contribution (tongues, spontaneous prayers, requests for choruses);
> lapsing into the jargon that haunts charismatic circles ("Shall we *just* pray?"—"God's timing is *always* right"—"A *wonderful* thing happened to me last week.")

The advice of trusted friends is to be coveted by a leader. They can point out distracting mannerisms and errors of judgment in leading a meeting. Although no leader needs a lengthy post-mortem after every meeting, it is useful from time to time to examine a particular meeting in some detail afterwards and discuss with the core group what can be learned from it. Through this continuous process of learning, the leader gradually puts himself more into the hands of God. Then, with experience, he becomes increasingly sensitive to the Holy Spirit's prompting. He can be alert to those surprises of the Spirit that so often bring a meeting to life—inviting the stranger in the third row to come forward and share something with the meeting because he (the leader) has a hunch that the stranger can do this; thinking of the most appropriate scripture to recite or chorus to sing at the moment of devotional climax in a meeting; offering a special ministry in an unpremeditated way because he has an inner prompting that someone is present who is longing for that kind of help.

One of the most memorable prayer meetings I took part in was arranged in a town in the south of England. The meeting-place was a large hall with a gallery—a former Methodist church—and gatherings of this kind were arranged in it about six times a year by a core group representing several of the congregations in the town. I went along as a casual visitor with a friend who lived nearby. We got to the hall about a quarter-of-an-hour before the meeting was due to commence to find that it was already half-full. A guitar group on one side of the platform led the singing, their leader encouraging the people by beating time with his hands. We were handed a chorus-book and ushered into the vacant seats. The warm-up was evidently an opportunity for personal choices, for the group on the platform invited people to call out the numbers of the choruses they wished to sing.

The meeting began when half-a-dozen men and women filed onto the platform and sat in a shallow semi-circle facing the auditorium. As the singing died away a tall man—the minister of the local Baptist church—stepped forward to the microphone and welcomed us to another "All Saints' Night". The saints, he said, were the people of God from the different congregations in the town got together to praise the name of Jesus Christ. (Murmurs of "Yes, yes" and "Praise the Lord!") Most of those present would know those who were with him on the platform (I gathered they were either clergy or laity from local churches in the neighbourhood) but among them was tonight's guest speaker, who stood up briefly and was greeted with a ripple of applause.

Now, the leader went on, looking round the hall, there were about four hundred present and he wanted them to identify themselves. Hands up those who are Church of England (about a third raised their hands), Methodists (about a tenth), Roman Catholics (also about a tenth) and so on. At the end of the roll-call, the leader invited one of the men on the platform to say the opening prayer. That individual said something like this:

"Heavenly Father, you gather your people together to hear your commandments and to praise your glorious name. Send your Holy Spirit upon us tonight. May he touch our hearts in penitence and cleanse us from all sin. We ask you to forgive us for being disobedient to you, in different ways, during this day. May we know your love, manifested through the cross of your Son Jesus Christ. Anoint those who will lead the worship—the speaker, the group, the one who presides, and all those whom you will summon to take a personal part in it. Open our lips to praise you, Lord."

Murmurs of "Amen" and "Yes, Lord," rose from the people around us. Whispered mutterings indicated that some were praying in tongues quietly. The sounds surged up in volume until everybody, as if directed by an unseen choirmaster, joined in a chorus:

> *Father, we adore you,*
> *lay our lives before you.*
> *How we love you!*

The assembly stood. The choruses poured out, one side of the auditorium following the other in a round. Eventually the crescendo faded away into a soft "Amen".

When we had resumed our seats the leader said he wanted to introduce to us someone he met just before the meeting who had been helped by the Lord in a remarkable way. A woman came forward and spoke into the microphone. She was nervous and hesitant at first, but seemed to be given confidence and eloquence as she unfolded her story. For several years she had suffered with a deteriorating condition in her spine. Her doctor had said there was nothing more that could be done for her medically. Then, a few weeks ago, she had received the laying on of hands for healing and her back immediately began to improve. Last week an X-ray at the hospital revealed a completely healed spine. She almost broke down at that point, and there were many cries of "Praise the Lord!" A man from the meeting joined her at the microphone. He was, he said, the woman's doctor and he wanted to testify briefly that the only explanation he had for her condition was that she had been touched by the healing hand of Jesus Christ himself. The two left the platform to further murmurs of praise.

The leader was obviously moved by the woman's testimony—as indeed, we all were. He suggested that we should praise God for what we had heard. A wave of thankfulness rippled through the meeting. Someone chanted a psalm, others joining in as they remembered the verses. A man spoke in tongues and another interpreted—the interpretation was a litany of thanksgiving to Jesus Christ for the salvation which he brought to mankind. More choruses were sung spontaneously, the guitar group accompanying the singing. Then there was a long silence. We felt our own hearts lifted up to God. The leader broke the silence by telling us that this testimony and praise should prepare us for the Word of God. The subject of tonight's talk was inner healing, he said, for salvation meant the healing of the whole personality. Another man on the platform stepped forward and read the story of the healing of the paralysed man in Mark 2.

After a song about Christ's healing power, sung as a solo by a girl from the music group, the leader invited the visiting speaker to the microphone. He was a Roman Catholic priest from the United States who had a wide knowledge of the ministry of inner healing. He drew for us a picture of healing in all its aspects—not just the healing of physical defects and diseases, but also the healing of hurts caused by sin and by weaknesses in an individual's personality, rooted in unresolved conflicts and memories of bitter relationships with parents and others in childhood days. He illustrated his theme from the lives of those he had counselled and focussed what he had to say on the double healing of the paralytic in the gospel—the forgiveness of sins and the restoration of the body. He spoke with such grace and authority that we did not notice an hour-and-a-half had slipped by.

When he had finished, the leader suggested that we should minister to one another in small groups. We were to greet two or three people sitting near us and then stand with them and pray as the Lord led us. Some people in the meeting looked embarrassed, not knowing what to do, but others clustered round them, and soon everyone was involved. In the group I joined, one wanted prayer for the healing of a persistent headache and another asked us to intercede for a son who was being interviewed for a job the next day. The words for these prayers came easily to our lips. As we stood together, I was conscious of dozens of others doing the same beyond our little circle, some with the laying on of hands, others with handshakes or arms round shoulders.

After about twenty minutes the leader called us to return to our places. Those who required further ministry should wait behind afterwards, he said, and there would be someone to talk to them. Finally, he announced the last chorus.

We left the hall about two and a half hours after we had entered.

Many of those who attend charismatic prayer meetings did so

initially because they were attracted by the atmosphere of praise. But as they begin to respond to God more freely in their own lives and to be open to the movement of the Holy Spirit in the meetings, they discover a deeper joy in the realisation that God is God and that he is to be worshipped with the whole of themselves. The actual events in the prayer meetings—the choruses, the speaker, the ministry—become very secondary. What is important is that worshippers are conscious of meeting Jesus in his Church and beyond his Church. Praise brings them to the threshold of heaven itself. To use the language of traditional Christian spirituality, they experience an exercise in corporate contemplation and find profound satisfaction in that alone. The prayer meeting, therefore, offers to the modern churchgoer a means of spiritual communion with God that is not encouraged much in the denominations today, except where a minority go away for quiet days and retreats.

So it is a mistake to dismiss the *Alleluias* of the charismatics and their singing in the Spirit as mere forms of youthful exuberance by those who are spiritually immature. Such expressions can begin in that way, of course, but if they are nothing more than signs of emotional release, they will not last long. Christians praise God because they learn to empty themselves before him and glimpse a meaning behind the apostle's words, "It is no longer I who live, but Christ who lives in me" (Galatians 2. 20). And when that happens, we are glad to sing praises. Yet we don't have to be vocal all the time. Our exultation may equally be expressed in utter silence. When God's people lift their hearts to him and know their union with him in Jesus Christ through the Holy Spirit, it does not matter whether they shout the words of the psalmist or breathe them quietly in silent adoration:

'Thou art holy,
        enthroned on the praises of Israel'

(Psalm 22.3)

4

The Prayer Group

A charismatic prayer group is formed when a small number of
those who have been baptised in the Holy Spirit, or who are
seeking to be open to Spirit-baptism, meet regularly at weekly or
fortnightly intervals. Sometimes the members will come from one
congregation, sometimes from two or more local churches.
Groups originate in many different ways. But always in those who
come there is a longing to be more aware of God's presence in
their lives, and a realisation that for them this is most likely to
happen in companionship with others.

This kind of group is rarely larger than ten or a dozen people.
Once a gathering grows there is a tendency to split into sub-
groups, for we cannot relate with the same degree of openness to
more than a few people at a time. And the charismatic prayer
group does encourage a family-like openness among its members.
The process of learning more about God's will for us as individuals means that we have to be prepared to let others help us at a
deeply personal level, and this process is hindered when the group
is either too large or its membership constantly changing. In
sociological terms the group becomes a "basic community". We
shall explore the implications of this within the relationships that
make up a local church in a later chapter.

High on the group's agenda for their meetings is reflection on
passages from the Bible. Christ who reveals the Father to us, saves
us and baptises us in his Spirit, is not a Christ of our own making.
He is the Christ who, in Calvin's phrase, is "clothed with his
Gospel". The Spirit quickens in the members of the group a desire
to be better acquainted with and obedient to the Word of God.
The resources of scholarship help us to understand the scriptures
in their own context, but renewing things only happen to Christians when the Word of God is trustfully acted upon. So in the

group we read a passage aloud, ponder over it in silence, discuss it, and reflect with one another on what God is saying to us through it. The Pentecostal gift of a word of wisdom sometimes dazzles our understanding. The charism may come through a member whom we do not expect to have such a knowledge: the man whose biblical fundamentalism is difficult for us to accept, or the woman who never reads anything more theological than the vicar's letter in the parish magazine. Theirs are "words not taught by human wisdom but taught by the Spirit, interpreting spiritual truths to those who possess the Spirit" (I Corinthians 2.13).

Among all but evangelical Christians there is a widespread ignorance of how the Holy Spirit uses the Bible as a means of speaking to us. Religious instruction in schools and scripture courses for adults in evening colleges are usually focussed on understanding the historical and exegetical problems surrounding the books of the Old and New Testaments; they take the sacred writings out of that environment of faith and prayer within which they become vehicles of the Word of God. Consequently the Bible tends to be a book full of comforting stories and mysterious doctrines rather than food for spiritual growth. I have often seen committed, devout churchgoers fumbling through the pages of a Bible and stumbling through some passage without any idea of how they might use its verses and its message to begin their prayers. I have also seen such people develop over months and years in their appreciation of the scriptures as they discovered how to open themselves to God's Word.

One man came into a charismatic prayer group that I led shortly after his conversion and confirmation in the Church of England. Except for what he had picked up during his attendance at church services and confirmation classes over six months, he knew nothing about the scriptures. After being a member of the group for about a year, he decided he could make little progress in his Christian life until he had familiarised himself with the scriptures, and he enrolled for a tough, two-year course at a Bible college in London. Those of us who knew him saw him not only grow in faith as he attended this course; his thinking, his speaking and his writing gradually became more scriptural in the sense that biblical concepts began to mould his outlook on life. He started interpreting events in terms of God's will and activity as the scriptures do, and he slowly found himself testing what he saw and heard around him—in the congregation itself as well as in the wider society within which he lived and worked—against the teaching of Jesus Christ as recorded in the gospels. It was a healthy experience for me, as an Anglican priest, to find myself challenged from time to time by one whom I had known as an unbeliever, but who was now increasing rapidly in spiritual stature through his membership of a prayer group and his disciplined reading of the Bible.

The group's reflections are not necessarily limited to the scriptures. Other books, articles from newspapers and magazines, cassettes—all these can provide material for this part of the agenda. But the group will turn back to the Bible like the point of a compass swinging round to magnetic north, for this is how we take our spiritual bearings. We shall find the Bible speaking to us with a directness and an authority that we hardly ever heard before when we studied it at school or heard it read in church.

From reflection on the scriptures we move on to the next item on the group's agenda—sharing. The prayer group provides us with an opportunity to share with others various things about our Christian lives—feelings and thoughts, questions and difficulties, experiences and hopes. This is essential for any real growth among Christians. Although we attend church services, we tend to isolate much of our spiritual lives—perhaps only saying a few words to the pastor when we find our prayers empty, or discussing with others a point from a sermon that we didn't understand. Sharing of a more deliberate and open nature encourages and hastens spiritual growth and is therefore one of our major resources for Christian living. The prayer group provides an admirable opportunity for sharing because the people who come expect it—they want to know how baptism in the Holy Spirit is to be related to their lives as Christians and how to go on from the experience of renewal to deeper commitment to Christ.

Sharing builds up our faith. When I hear from others how God is working in their daily lives, I am reminded of his love for me and of his invitation to me to put more trust in him. Over a number of years there have been times when I was a member of a closely-knit Christian group, and there have been other times when I wasn't. I've no doubt which were the more spiritually strengthening as far as I was concerned. When I haven't been part of a sharing group, it has been much more difficult to be aware of the Lord's presence and activity in my life. I have found difficulty in discerning his will without the help of others, and I have wanted to do things my way instead of his.

Receiving and giving encouragement to one another helps us to grow in holiness. Many of us have a poor self-image. Things have been said and done in the past that create an impression that we are not much good either as human beings or as Christians. The poison of self-hatred may have been injected into us by our home, school and work environments, and this poison can be intensified by a preaching of salvation that has stressed our worthlessness without equally stressing our status in Christ as sons of God baptised in his Spirit. Affection and encouragement from others sets us free from the effects of this and helps us to concentrate our attention on serving the Lord. The more we learn to support one another, the more our ingrained sense of independence will be replaced by a healthier Christian sense of interdependence. As I move round various charismatic prayer groups, I notice how readily support is asked for and freely given in spiritual as well as in material needs. It extends even to the practice of ringing up other members of the group during the day and asking for prayer when one is facing a particular difficulty or challenge.

Hearing others speak of their love for the Lord and confessing their personal weaknesses and disobediences encourages us to be open with them, too. We also speak about our temptations and failures because we know the group will listen with understanding and sympathy. Wisely, the Church has officially discouraged public confessions of actual sins of an intimate nature. But sometimes it is right to admit a particular fault and to ask the group to pray that we may be given grace to overcome it. The love and prayer of the group after such an admission is a powerful reassurance of the lovingkindness of God. When members can be even more honest and express their adverse feelings for one another, and accept each other in love afterwards, then they are growing in corporate strength.

Sharing in concern for one another thus moves into prayer —the third item on the group's agenda. Together we turn to the Lord with our problems, our requests, our fears, our hopes. For many this is a new experience of prayer. Many regular church-goers have never developed beyond the stage of simple petitionary prayer. Perhaps when they were children they adopted a pattern of devotion and have never advanced beyond that early stereotype. I have met middle-aged and even elderly Christians who still say the same prayers by their bedside at night that they said when they were twelve or fourteen years old. By its very nature formal worship is not always able to help them. The prayers that are said publicly have to be of a general kind, and it is not easy to adapt them to individual needs in the congregation beyond mentioning the names of the sick. Consequently church-goers do not expect the prayers of other Christians to be imme-diately relevant to their personal needs. During the service there may be a sentence in the sermon that brings them comfort, or a phrase in a hymn, psalm or prayer; but it is likely that they will be more encouraged by the few words that they have with the pastor at the door afterwards than anything that was said or sung in church.

In the group we gradually begin to offer to God the confessions, the requests, the thanksgivings and the praises that the Holy Spirit prompts within us. We embark on an adventure in prayer, push-ing out into those mysterious waters that we once thought belonged only to the saints. We become bolder pray-ers. We ask in confidence that God will hear; we praise with the knowledge that he will shape our words. Gifts of tongues, interpretations and simple prophecies make us aware of the voice of the risen Lord in our midst. Personal crises caused by anxieties, bitterness, grief, and damaged relationships are presented for the ministry of the Church's intercession, and they are caught up in the rhythm of the group's devotions. We experience God's guidance, healing and grace through the group as we walk through these dark valleys. We don't need much encouragement to pray when this is our experience. Prayer becomes infinitely worthwhile; it is the heart-beat of the Christian fellowship, and our own hearts beat with it.

Alongside our own dependence upon the group for their minis-try to us, there gradually arises a realisation that we can be used in ministry to them. We discover how the gifts of the Spirit are God's equipment to us for this purpose. The group encourages us to take the first hesitant steps. Usually a member will say that he has a problem that he would like us to pray for. We have never done this before, but nervously we speak a few words in prayer for him. To our astonishment, the words we utter make sense, even though we were too startled to think about them, and the member seems to have been helped. We are even more astonished when, a few days later, he tells us our prayer for him has been answered.

The vocal charisms are usually the first we exercise. We pray aloud in tongues—and we are delighted when someone interprets. Another time we attempt an interpretation. After a few words, our voice falters and we make a mess of it, but the group accepts this and urges us to try again. The next time our words are more in tune with our inner response to God. We are learning how to fix our attention on him and not on our listeners. Our confidence increases because we know that what we say is being tested by the group.

Other spiritual gifts, such as a word of knowledge in counselling, a gift of healing, a discernment of spirits, or an act of deliverance, have been given to Christians as they began to minister to one another in a charismatic prayer group. When you enter into a ministry for another, it almost always involves taking a risk—being willing to speak when the inclination is powerful and seems to come from God, being willing to lay hands on someone and claim healing or deliverance with the authority of Christ. But you are willing to take such risks in a group like this, for you have the security of knowing that, if you make a mistake, no one is going to regard it as a disaster.

In this way all members of the group learn to participate, not only in discussions on the Bible, personal sharing and prayer, but also in ministry to one another. The participation by all in the life of the group is of immense importance to its dynamics. Each is called on to contribute, and this gives everyone the experience of ministering to others in the power of the Spirit in a way that is not often possible in ordinary congregations. Among the classical Pentecostal Churches this is known as "an every-member ministry". Although the teaching is clearly presented in the New Testament, it has been obscured in the mainline denominations by the development of a professional class of "ministers". The common attitude among churchgoers is that the Church's "ministry", in the restricted sense of service to others in spiritual things, is the responsibility of the clergy. The fact that many functions such as preaching, leading services, and administering the sacraments are usually performed by those who are ordained has strengthened this attitude. The Pentecostals avoided this distortion through the circumstances within which their denomination originated in the

United States. Reacting against what they regarded as the unscriptural institutionalism of the mainline denominations, they rejected any kind of ordained ministry and relied on the immediate power of the Holy Spirit available to each baptised member. Fundamentalists in doctrine, they expected the ministries listed in the New Testament to rise up through spiritual gifts in each congregation. It was their sincere belief that every member was a minister that resulted in their remarkable growth as a denomination during this century, in spite of their unhappy tendency to fragment into different groups.

The concept of an every-member ministry has been taught in the denominations for many years, though usually under the name of "lay ministry" or "lay apostolate". But the charismatic movement, bringing a new realisation of what it means to be baptised in the Holy Spirit and a new opportunity for ministry to others through the gifts of the Spirit, especially in small prayer groups, has made the concept more real in the experience of ordinary churchgoers. To be a Christian who ministers is now more than just organising a stewardship campaign or training as a lay preacher: it can mean speaking a prophetic word in the name of Jesus Christ, laying hands on a sick person for healing, and claiming the victory of the cross for one caught in an evil snare. Preaching, teaching, counselling, healing, evangelism, leading in prayer—these are no longer the special responsibility of the ordained clergy, except in certain situations where Church order should be respected. They can be the ministry of any Christian with the Holy Spirit's gift.

My own understanding of this was enlightened by an incident in the first charismatic prayer group of which I was a member. We met each week on Tuesday evenings from nine o'clock until about midnight (my duties as a parish priest prevented me from arriving earlier, and it was convenient for one or two members to come after their children had gone to bed). One Tuesday I had an attack of influenza. I ought not to have gone out, but for some reason I was prompted to attend the prayer group as usual. The others noted my condition and sympathised. When we commenced the prayers, a young wife in the group came and stood behind my chair, laid her hands on my head, and asked the Lord to heal me. It was the first time I had received such a ministry—indeed, except for the bishops who laid hands on me when I was confirmed and ordained, I do not think I had been prayed for in this manner previously. Certainly not by a woman! The next morning, when I woke up, the 'flu had disappeared. I was feeling fine, without even a trace of a headache. I would never have believed that an ordinary member of the congregation could have been used in ministry in this way if I had not experienced such a blessing!

The ministry of the leader is no less important in the charismatic prayer group than in the charismatic prayer meeting. Caring for members of the group, encouraging first one and then the other to exercise a gift or embark on a ministry, suggesting what fresh initiatives should be explored, supervising the wise discerning of spirits, making the dozen-and-one practical arrangements to keep the group together—these make up the ministry of the group leader (or leaders, if the task is shared). The style of leadership is different from that exercised in a prayer meeting—not of firm control but of enabling presence—but the result is the same. The leader helps the group and the individuals in it to grow in the Lord. Training courses for leaders involving experiences in group dynamics, partnership with other leaders, and lectures on the science of human behaviour, can assist individuals in this ministry, but I suspect that all real leaders are gifted by God rather than coached by men. If the charism is absent, the leadership that is exercised will be second-best.

There is much more that could be said about these groups. Not everything that is experienced within them is sweetness and light! Most groups have problems from time to time—within themselves, with pastors and congregations.* This is why Spirit-gifted leadership is so important. It provides the simple structure for the group within which these problems can be sorted out and members can form a lively cell within the local church.

The charismatic prayer group, then, is a very different kind of animal from most of the groups that are associated with local churches—the sub-committee, the Bible reading circle, the confirmation class, and the women's guild. Although the members of a prayer group may not be consciously aware of this difference at first, it gradually dawns on them that what they are experiencing is a deeper quality in their relationships as Christians than that which they find elsewhere. This is why a well-led, gifted prayer

* See my *Charismatic Prayer Group: A Handbook for Leaders, Members and Clergy* (Hodder and Stoughton, 1975).

group becomes so important to them. Just as the charismatic prayer meeting opens up for them new visions of what it means to worship the Lord, so the charismatic prayer group gives them new ideas of what it means to be in fellowship with one another in his Spirit.

5

Preparation for Renewal

"How can we bring renewal to our church?"

I have often been asked this question, by laity as well as clergy—by Anglicans, Evangelicals, Methodists and Lutherans as well as Reformed, Baptists, Roman Catholics and even Pentecostals! When I was a parish priest I used to ask the question myself! What's the technique? Do we organise courses on the gifts of the Spirit, introduce choruses to Sunday worship, and urge the congregation to go to charismatic meetings? Many possibilities flit through our minds. When we listen to talks given by those who have experienced the renewing power of the Spirit in their local churches, or when we read books written by them about it, we feel a mixture of hope and despair. If only the same thing would happen in our church!

But behind the question as I have set it is a basic error. That error is revealed in the first three words: *How can we . . .? We* cannot plan when and how renewal will come to our church. It is only God who can renew his people. What we have to do is to prepare ourselves for his coming.

Such preparation usually consists of three things:

(1) Prayer by a group within the congregation who see that prayer as part of their commitment to the whole membership,

(2) Teaching made available for everyone, and

(3) Opportunities for the members of the congregation to experience worship that includes features we are learning within the charismatic movement.

The particular moment when one or more of these can be initiated in a local church is a matter for prayerful discernment. The golden rule is to make haste slowly. Take the formation of the prayer group, for example. It does not usually happen successfully if a member of the congregation starts pestering the others that they ought to form one. The best prayer groups that I have known often seem to have sprung up in a spontaneous way. Someone has a feeling of dissatisfaction because of his own spiritual weakness. He casually mentions this to one or two others to discover that they have similar feelings about themselves, and suddenly they find themselves coming together to pray about it. Sometimes the pastor receives indications that there are folk in the church who are beginning to thirst for more of God in their lives—murmurs about their ineffectiveness as Christians, requests for help in praying, major problems or minor tragedies in their lives that cause them to look for God's grace. Things like these are like the first rustles from the leaves on the tree that tell us the wind is beginning to stir.

Prayer by a group committed to a local church is often the lengthiest part of the preparation for renewal. It can stretch out for a number of years. I have been to several churches where a few people met weekly or fortnightly, usually with their pastor, to seek God's will for themselves and for the congregation of which they were members, and then had to wait a long time before they saw any answer to their prayers. To start with such groups have little idea why they meet. They are confused and unsure of themselves. All that brings them together is a vague hunch that one day the Lord will use them. They read the Bible, pass round books on renewal, attend some charismatic meetings in the neighbourhood, and stumble through the first acts of corporate prayer. They have relationship problems. Two or three members grow weary and cease to attend. The rest of the congregation regard them with indifference, tolerant amusement or suspicion. But they go on meeting, and the day comes when they realise that their numbers are growing, and a quickening concern for the things of God is evident among others in the congregation.

A prayer group like this is a seed-bed of congregational renewal. Inevitably at the beginning there is a sense of exclusiveness about it, because not all the members of a local church will want to join in. When the numbers attending increase, it may be necessary to divide into two or more groups, who perhaps come together occasionally to form a prayer meeting. Charismatic prayer groups and prayer meetings that spring up within a local church in this way, drawing the majority of their participants from one congregation, have an immense value. They are then accepted as indigenous activities within the congregation rather than activities that have been imported from outside.

The second thing I mentioned, teaching, is essential for there is much ignorance of and misunderstanding about the renewal movement. Charismatics tend to forget this. Since they go to renewal meetings and read books, they become fairly well-informed about topics such as the gifts of the Holy Spirit. But not the average churchgoer in most of the denominations. For him Pentecostalism is just one more in a bewildering variety of -isms, and the treatment given to the topic by the news media is usually distorting, especially when exorcisms are involved.

It is important to set the charismatic renewal within the wider horizon of all that the Church teaches about God's saving work through his Son Jesus Christ and his election of his people. This is a vast subject and only the briefest of outlines can be given here. Generally speaking, recent theology has tended to interpret the nature of the Church as in some sense continuing the mystery of Christ's incarnation. The Christian life is a personal entry into the life, death and resurrection of Jesus, and the Word of God continues to be incarnated in the lives of Christians today. As a result of this theological trend, the image of the Church as the body of Christ has risen above other scriptural images (or "models" as they are more often called nowadays) and much of the Church's life—worship, sacraments, fellowship, structure, preaching, mission, ecumenism—is interpreted exclusively in "body of Christ" terms.

Without in any way diminishing this model, it should be pointed out that it is only one among several in the scriptures, and to teach a concept of the Church which relates its members only to the mystery of the incarnation through the use of that one model, without at the same time relating them through other models to the mystery of Pentecost, restricts the fullness of the Word of God. It is like celebrating the festivals of the incarnation in the Church's year (Christmas, Epiphany, Holy Week, Easter and Ascension) without celebrating the festival of the gift of the Holy Spirit (Pentecost). Jesus Christ was anointed by the Holy Spirit (at his baptism in the river Jordan, the ancient theme of the feast of Epiphany) to proclaim the kingdom of God and to fulfil the mission on which he had been sent by the Father. This mission was fulfilled in the shedding of his blood on Calvary, and vindicated in his resurrection and enthronement at the Father's right hand. Through him the Father promised and sent the Holy Spirit on the disciples to continue the mission of Christ in Jesus' name. The Spirit is still sent on Christ's disciples today. In teaching the meaning of Pentecost, the established denominations have often been vague because they have been unsure of themselves, or have interpreted the Holy Spirit's work solely in terms of God's authority and power in certain institutions (the sacraments, the ordained ministry, the authorised formularies). That is why classical Pentecostals proudly affirm that they preach the *full* Gospel.

A deeper appreciation of the Spirit's anointing, however, leads us to see more clearly how the Church is constituted by God. The imaginary TV picture in a previous chapter, showing people coming together under the impulse of the Spirit, illustrated a theological truth that has been neglected. It is that to be a member of the body of Christ is to be united with the incarnate Lord *through the outpouring of the Holy Spirit*. We are not made Christians only through repentance and faith, nor are we made Christians only by baptism. Fundamentally it is the work of the Spirit in our lives *now* that makes us Christians, followers of the *Christos*, the "anointed one". Repentance and faith are given by the Spirit, and baptism in water is made an effective sacramental sign by him; but in the end repentance, faith and baptism are the conditions under which God elects us: the agent of grace is his Spirit. This is basic scriptural teaching, and those who discuss the charismatic renewal should have no difficulty in showing how the lessons of the renewal flow within the main current of orthodox Christian doctrine. It is then necessary to develop this instruction in showing that the giving of the Holy Spirit who constitutes the Church may be understood in two closely interrelated aspects.

The first aspect of the Spirit's work in a Christian's life is to give each one of us a personal knowledge of God and of his love for us, demonstrated supremely in the passion and death of his Son. God is love, and he calls each human person into a communion of love with himself in Christ. This cannot be achieved by man's effort but is brought about by the free gift of the Spirit through Christ, communicating God's life and love to him. The Spirit thus brings us into an experiential awareness of God, centred at the root level of our consciousness, which is deeper than thought or feeling. Without this personal assurance, such knowledge of God as we might attain would remain simply knowledge *about* God and would be purely intellectual. Only the Spirit can bring us into living communion with God. When we experience this living communion with him, it will lead to an inner transformation and eventually there will be reflected in our lives the character of Jesus Christ, the fruit of the Spirit.

The second aspect of the Holy Spirit's work is to equip us for the mission of Jesus Christ in the world. Just as an experience of human love will often draw out new gifts and resources from the one who knows that he or she is loved, so an awareness of God's love will bring forth in us fresh powers and vitality. The more we experience God's love, the more our life becomes gifted for others. "God's love has been poured into our hearts through the Holy Spirit which has been given to us" (Romans 5.5). The fruit and the gifts of the Spirit are the expressions of God's love through the lives of his people. "Without the full complement of the fruit and gifts of the Spirit, God's love is incomplete to and through his Church. With the present outpouring of the Holy Spirit we are seeing the Spirit of love completing his ministry in the Church. This is how the Church is to become as fresh and full of promise as the morning; as fair as the still, cool beauty of the moon; as bright as the warm revealing sun; and as terrible as an aggressive victorious army with banners" (Song of Solomon 6.10).*

In the early years of the charismatic movement teaching was usually based on the speaker's own experience of baptism in the Holy Spirit and ministry through his charisms. "A few personal recollections and half-a-dozen jokes," as I once heard these addresses described. There will always be a place for personal testimony in teaching, but theological reflection on our experiences is vital. Unless we are prepared to test our experiences alongside the Church's traditional and unfolding understanding of the truth as revealed in Jesus Christ, we shall become hopelessly subjective and prone to error. Early speakers and writers in the movement took over uncritically some of the teachings of classical Pentecostals without exploring further their scriptural and doctrinal bases. Now a theology of the charismatic renewal is gradually

* Robert C. Frost, *Overflowing Life* (Logos International, 1971, p. 127).

taking shape as gifted scholars—often themselves being baptised in the Holy Spirit—relate the experiences of thousands of Christians to the Church's teaching.

In England the Fountain Trust has promoted instruction about the charismatic renewal through meetings, conferences, the magazine *Renewal* and other publications. The Community of Celebration at Post Green, Lytchett Minster, Dorset, sends out teams to teach "various aspects of the Spirit-filled life in the context of a church coming alive in the Spirit" (to quote from its brochure). Teaching is also given by communities whose corporate lives are powerful media for their message, such as the Barnabas Fellowship at Whatcombe House near Blandford in Dorset and Fellowship House, Pilgrims Hatch, Brentwood in Essex. In the United States the Catholic Charismatic Renewal Services and other bodies work in a similar way through communities, conferences, teaching teams and publications such as the magazine *New Covenant*. American Catholics have devised a series of *Life in the Spirit* seminars which are used all over the world to help Christians who are seeking release in the Spirit.

Inspired teaching is one of the charisms that God gives his Church, and it was never more needed than today. Christians long to be better instructed. The short sermonette at the parish eucharist or the family service has left many with only a kindergarten knowledge of their faith. When a man or a woman, anointed with the spiritual gift of teaching, presents Jesus Christ as the living Lord of the Church, modern audiences will listen eagerly. Whatever educationalists tell us about peoples' inability to listen to more than a few minutes' talk, I have to say that I have been to numerous meetings where charismatic speakers have held the attention of large audiences for an hour or more.

But teaching about the charismatic movement without some experience of charismatic ways of worship is like hearing a description of a beauty spot without ever visiting it. That is why it is not a very suitable topic to be presented in a twenty minutes' lecture at an ecclesiastical synod or the annual general meeting of a church society! So I have listed, as the third part of a congregation's preparation for renewal, opportunities to experience worship that incorporates features we are learning from Pentecostalism.

Quite often, after a period of teaching and discussion, people in a local church will begin to say, "Don't just talk about it! Show us!" (or words to that effect). That indicates the time has arrived to introduce them, with great sensitivity and patience, to charismatic worship. It may be that the core group organises a series of prayer meetings to which those interested can be invited. If the core group has begun to experience the Pentecostal gifts in their own prayers together, they will be alert to the possibility of using them in a larger meeting. In an assembly of fifty or sixty, six or eight can lead the rest into more charismatic worship.

Local churches can help one another. Eighteen people from a Church of England parish in Manchester spent a long weekend with another parish in Durham. The visitors stayed in the homes of the members of the Durham parish and joined in their worship and activities. The effect was remarkable. The eighteen came back to Manchester knowing they had experienced the love and power of God in his Church in a new way, and they longed for their own congregation to be more open to the Spirit.

Individuals and teams, such as those I have just named, are available to spend weekends in local churches to teach about renewal in the Spirit. Charismatic fellowships have been set up in towns and cities to provide a means for several congregations to join in the project. The Saturday afternoon and evening is spent in giving talks, answering questions, and leading a session of prayer and praise. The team is then involved in the Sunday services, preaching and leading the worship. On the Monday morning there is a seminar for the clergy. The value of involving several neighbouring congregations in a project like this is that people then realise how widespread is the desire among Christians for renewal—especially if the congregations belong to different denominations.

Weekend conferences can also help a congregation to grow together and to become more sensitive to the leading of the Spirit. Guest speakers who have a wide experience of charismatic ways can minister on these occasions by encouraging and teaching those who attend. There is something about living, working and praying together that assists a congregation to realise its fellowship in Jesus Christ in a way that is rarely achieved in years of coming together for services on Sundays. Even if they are only in a conference centre from Friday evening until Sunday afternoon, they have an experience of community that points them to the

Holy Spirit who builds them into the Church. There is no set pattern for weekends like these, but they usually include one or two sessions of free praise and spontaneous prayer, and they end with a eucharist on the Sunday afternoon. Churchgoers who are used only to formal worship find it easier to relax into different modes of intercession, penitence and praise away from the atmosphere of a church building.

It is sometimes possible to make the subject of charismatic renewal the focus of a teaching week within a local church. In the spring of 1976 I was invited with my wife, Margaret, to spend three weeks at St. Philip's Anglican Church, Montreal West, Canada, to introduce the topic to the whole congregation. A number of people there had been involved in the charismatic renewal for some time and there was widespread interest among others in the congregation.

In 1974 the rector of St. Philip's, Ian Stuchbery, his wife, Sylvia, and a number of the congregation had begun meeting on Wednesday evenings each week for Bible study and prayer. During the next few months the number of those attending grew to about twenty-five. Some arrived at the parish hall about six o'clock for a meal together. Others came an hour later. Two groups were formed, one to seek baptism in the Spirit through a *Life in the Spirit* seminar, the other to explore related topics. The groups came together for prayer and praise at about eight o'clock and the evening ended with an informal eucharist. After about a year, many of those who came on Wednesday evenings spent a weekend on a farm to pray about the future, and it seemed as if the Lord was telling them that the time had come for them to organise a teaching week for the whole congregation on the subject of charismatic renewal. It was then that Ian decided to invite me and my wife to travel to Canada to conduct it.

As we planned the teaching week in letters across the Atlantic, we saw it take shape in two stages—first a week of preparation for the Wednesday evening core group before the actual teaching week itself (the fact that a cheaper fare was available if Margaret and I stayed twenty-one days helped us to see this!). In the first week the core group would be helped to be more committed to Jesus Christ themselves and to learn more of what charismatic renewal meant for the Church; in the second week I, with them, would open the subject up for the congregation.

The day before we arrived in Canada one of the leading members of the core group, Court Baker, a branch manager in an insurance company, was taken into hospital in Montreal with a suspected thrombosis of a vein at the back of an eye. Tests were performed, and he was advised by the surgeon that he would be operated on in a day or two. The purpose of the operation was to open an artery in his neck and to clean it out as it appeared from X-rays and scans to be blocked. Ian, Margaret, Bobs (Court's wife) and I visited him the day before the operation was due to take place. Some months later I asked Court to write an account of what happened:

"You came in on that Wednesday afternoon with Margaret, Bobs and Ian—quite a formidable bunch, to say the least!—and laid hands on me for healing. When the angiogram was done on the Thursday morning, I asked the doctor how my pipes looked and he said, 'I wish mine were that open!' Later, a very puzzled surgeon visited my room and said he didn't think surgery would be necessary. The next day it was confirmed that there was no need for an operation and that I could be discharged."

This gift of healing was immensely encouraging. The core group met most of the evenings of the following week, and we spent the whole of Saturday together. During those days I saw the Lord equipping twenty or so Christians to minister to others in his name. The group began to look outwards towards the congregation and the neighbourhood with a growing conviction that the Holy Spirit would use them in love and power. I do not think I am exaggerating when I say that if I had left Canada at the end of that week, the teaching week would have proceeded just as effectively—so great was the impetus given by God to that group.

The days of the teaching week were divided between meetings in church and meetings in houses. On the evenings of Sunday, Tuesday and Thursday, Margaret and I spoke to gatherings of between two hundred and thirty and two hundred and eighty in the church—the majority of those attending being members of the parish. On the evenings of Monday, Wednesday and Friday, Margaret, Ian and I spent about three-quarters-of-an-hour with nine groups in houses (we visited three each), answering questions and praying with them. Everyone who attended a meeting in church was invited to a house group. On the final Sunday evening we celebrated the eucharist in church with much praising, singing in the Spirit, a liturgical dance, and a joyful procession in which everyone joined.

The events of the teaching week made it possible for individual members of the congregation to be better informed about the charismatic movement, to raise their own questions in the informal setting of someone's home, and to experience both prayer in the small group and worship in church. By throwing the subject open to everyone, and by showing how many in the congregation had already been helped and blessed by God (Court's testimony of his healing created a deep impression), we managed to bury the rumour that the charismatic movement was an exclusive, exotic affair. It was explained that Christians all over the world, including some in Montreal, were experiencing the love and power of God in a new way in their lives, and that the charismatic group in St. Philip's were wanting to share this experience with all other members.

Six months after the teaching week, Ian reported in a letter: "All is progressing well. The house groups, having slumped during the summer (when everything stops in Canada!), are reviving and seven are meeting regularly, most of them every two weeks. In addition, a number of individuals get together to pray among themselves. The Wednesday evening programme continues to be a means of real strength to us. Despite some drawbacks (we've tried to control it rather too much!), we have felt the Holy Spirit to be among us. We have felt the need for more teaching and a good many are taking part in an adult confirmation class, an enquirers' group, and a *Life in the Spirit* seminar."

What happened at St. Philip's is not necessarily what could happen elsewhere. As I have said, each local church must seek the Lord's way for itself in introducing its membership to opportunities for renewal in the Holy Spirit. We must test our plans against the fundamental questions: Do they glorify God? Will they enable others to realise the love of Christ in the Church? During the final eucharist of the teaching week in Montreal, someone in the congregation cried out a word of wisdom: "God's love is for everybody!" It was a gracious reminder.

6

Pastoral Leadership

Some years ago a group of young people belonging to a large church near London became involved in charismatic renewal, many of them experiencing fresh dimensions of freedom and joy in their Christian lives. They began a weekly meeting and their numbers grew to sixty or seventy. Unfortunately these developments alarmed the pastor and the older members of the congregation, who questioned the validity of what the young people were experiencing. They dismissed the idea that Christians could be baptised in the Holy Spirit and said the young people were propagating unacceptable doctrines. Matters came to a head when the young people unwisely tried to enliven the Sunday worship with choruses and spontaneous praying. They acted more in a spirit of defiance than a spirit of love. The result was a bitter argument and eventually they left the congregation as a body, meeting for worship on their own in a hall they rented a few miles away. A shudder went round the neighbouring churches when the news of this reached them. "The charismatic movement is divisive," they said.

This is true—in one sense. Renewal in the Holy Spirit *is* divisive because of our unwillingness always to respond to God's call. Some will be more ready for his coming than others, and those who are hesitant will begin to feel separated from those who are trying to be obedient. The sayings of Jesus Christ about the divisiveness of the Second Coming—the wise and foolish maidens, the two women at the mill—are applicable to the coming of the Holy Spirit on a congregation in renewal. Not all are prepared to be open to him—at least, not initially.

But we must beware of attributing every indication of divisiveness simply to human weakness—to a rebellious spirit in some and a deafness to God's voice in others. Divisions can be caused by the immobility of the local church as an institution as well. The forces that combine to maintain the *status quo* in a congregation, as in the wider denomination, are powerful and resistant to change. People feel secure in fixed and familiar patterns. The general expectation of most people who attend churches is that the accepted norms will not be changed. Alterations disrupt what they are used to and challenge their basic assumptions.

Inertia like this within a congregation has a protective value. It is less likely to be swept along by the latest fashion. What is of value from its past and present customs is safeguarded. But no congregation can remain completely static. If Christian people are not being renewed in their commitment to God and to the mission on which he sends them in the world—with the changes in attitudes, policies and structures that this mission demands—then that congregation will grow old and weary. Its members will go down to their graves bound by traditions that died long ago. We find this pathetic state of affairs in those Christian groups in local churches that cling to forms of worship and mission that were manifestations of spiritual renewal during the last generation but one. Congregations need to be helped to discern where change is required and to accept it in obedience to God. Those who are fearful can be assured that when the Lord renews a local church, he does not usually ask it to make a complete break with its past. They can be shown that there is a continuity in God's dealings with his people through the years so that what emerges as new—in pastoral practice, in missionary strategy, in developing ministries and in forms of worship—will be a progression from what has gone before. In fact, discernment in the way God is leading us into the future is sharpened by our appreciation of how he has led us in former years.

The key figures in this process are those who exercise pastoral leadership within a congregation. Presiding over this leadership in most local churches is the ordained pastor—the parish priest, the rector, the vicar, the minister, or whatever he may be called. In his office he acts as a focus for the building up of the unity of the Christian body in that place, representing the congregation within the wider Church and the wider Church within the congregation. Therefore a special responsibility rests with him in guiding the local church through the tensions that renewal brings among the membership. (I am assuming that the pastor does, in fact, exercise an effective leadership within the local church. If he doesn't, then there is something wrong in that community, and before renewal can come that problem must be sorted out.)

At the service for the ordination of priests in the Church of England, the bishop asks the candidates:

"Will you maintain and set forwards, as much as lieth in you, quietness, peace, and love, among all Christian people, and especially among them that are or shall be committed to your charge?"

They answer: "I will so do, the Lord being my helper."

In the rubrics at the beginning of the Communion service the *Book of Common Prayer* gives the parish priest authority to intervene between those who would "not be persuaded to a godly unity".

Later on in the letter I received from Montreal, quoted in the last chapter, Ian Stuchbery wrote:

"One of the results (of the teaching week) has been something of a polarisation within the parish relating to (the charismatic meetings) on Wednesday nights. Undoubtedly a good deal of my interest and attention has been focussed on this part of our parish programme and other aspects of renewal. This has led to a rather vaguely defined section of the congregation feeling left out in the cold. They have not identified with what we are trying to encourage and have reacted by saying, 'The rector is only interested in those who go on Wednesday nights.' At the moment I am trying to show that this isn't true—firstly, by going out of my way to show concern for other aspects of parish life and, secondly, by urging those who are finding a new love and fellowship in the Spirit to be a real power of love and concern in the parish."

The way in which a pastor sets about this will depend to some extent on his own attitude towards the charismatic renewal. If he rejects it entirely on theological grounds, then he will be in no position to guide the members of his congregation. One Church of England vicar denounced from the pulpit the manifestations of renewal in other churches in the city and forbade his listeners to go to any meeting or to read any books on the topic! It need hardly be said that such an attitude created grave divisions in that congregation. On the other hand, a pastor who finds it difficult to sympathise with the principles of Pentecostalism but who exercises a sensitive care towards those who are involved in the renewal will be respected and his leadership valued.

Many clergy find themselves challenged by the movement, both in their personal lives and in their acceptance of the Gospel as they have learned it, and this sometimes accounts for the caution they show when charismatics in their congregation first approach them with enthusiastic suggestions. Anglican and Roman Catholic priests have been bred in a tradition which assumes spiritual initiatives should properly come from the clergy and, as I have described in my own experience, it takes time for them to realise that the Holy Spirit can move just as powerfully through the ministry of a layman as through the ministry of those who have been ordained! The expectations of their congregations are also limited in their views of their own and their pastor's ministries. When I first began inviting members of the congregation where I was vicar to do some of the things that had been done by my predecessors (like preparing candidates for confirmation and leading a Bible study group), others thought that I was shirking what I was trained and paid to do!

I think the charismatic renewal is helping us to clarify our ideas on what is the basic ministry of the pastor. This is a question that has perplexed many of the ordained in the denominations recently (see how a new book on this subject turns up in publishers' lists almost every year!). Through a deeper appreciation of the concept of an every-member ministry, the spiritual gift of the ordained minister is seen to be that of "presidency". He is not one who has every spiritual gift necessary for the congregation, nor is he necessarily a specialist in some of the functions that are normally attributed to him (for example, teaching or counselling). But what he has above all is the charism of leadership which enables him to preside over a congregation in its worship, life and mission, in such a way that he enables individuals and groups in that congregation to minister with the gifts that God gives them.

Of course, many clergy do have other special gifts as well as this basic one for presidency. The clergyman who finds himself increasingly employed in another ministry ought to consider whether or not he should relinquish his pastoral responsibility if the demands made on him for that other ministry are great. This is sometimes possible through the specialist posts set up within the denominations. And many clergy have to undertake ministries for which they are not equipped, simply because there is a need for them and there is no one else who can do them. If this happens, it should be regarded as a temporary expediency, to be dropped if it diverts the pastor from his basic task. When a pastor is himself being renewed by the Holy Spirit, he will find the spiritual gift of presidential leadership strengthened and enriched in him, and he will discover new gifts of discernment and wisdom enabling him to guide his congregation as it grows with a greater experience of God's grace.

With this comes a renewal in the pastor's authority. The spiritual gift fills out his office with the power that comes from God, and the members of the congregation begin to sense this. It throws into a right perspective the respect and submission that a congregation owes its leader. "We beseech you, brethren, to respect those who labour among you and are over you in the Lord," wrote the apostle (I Thessalonians 5.12). This is not to say that everyone in a congregation becomes a pastor's "yes-man". Nor is it a plea for a return to that paternalism that was characteristic of a clergyman's attitude towards his flock in bygone days. It is an acknowledgement that the pastor is equipped by the Holy Spirit to preside over the congregation and that in submitting to his ministry, the members of the congregation are submitting to God's gift. (I am assuming, of course, that the pastor is himself open to the Lord and is not exercising his office in an unworthy manner. How the members of a congregation act in the case of a pastor who is himself disobedient to God and to those over him is a different matter, involving the wider fellowship of the Church.)

Charismatics should remember this, especially if their pastor does not seem immediately enthusiastic about the movement for renewal. Rarely does any blessing come on a congregation when part of its membership is in rebellion against its pastor. The love of God does not flow through a rejection of his gifts. Six young couples belonging to a Church of England parish in East Anglia attended a series of renewal meetings in a neighbouring town and were baptised in the Holy Spirit. Then they went to see their vicar.

"We've come to let you know that we're completely committed to you and to your ministry here," they told the startled clergyman. "What do you want to do with us?"

That particular vicar had never heard of charismatic renewal (it was a *very* rural part of East Anglia!) But those words to that man was the beginning of a remarkable spiritual revival in that parish. It happened because the pastor recognised the love and support of the Lord in the people around him.

Except where congregations are tiny, the pastoral leadership in a local church is not vested solely in the ordained pastor. Other men and women contribute to the building up of the Church by the initiatives they take in various aspects of a congregation's life. They make suggestions, see opportunities, are sensitive to the needs and feelings of others, and have gifts that enable the congregation to be more effective in its witness and service. Without them others feel a sense of loss and of not belonging. They are known as "cohesive personalities" because they help the rest of the group to stick together and to work in harmony with one another. They help to create with the pastor a sense of solidarity among the faithful. The charismatic renewal is assisting us to recognise in these Christians spiritual gifts of leadership and to encourage them to fulfil their ministry in the congregation.

Most denominations have offices within their local church structures to give scope for this charism of leadership among their members. But in nearly every case the offices have tended to be held by those with administrative rather than pastoral responsibilities. Charismatic renewal in a United Reformed congregation in the north of England influenced the attitude of the elders to their responsibilities. Instead of seeing themselves as just a committee to discuss matters with their pastor and to support him in his ministry, they began to accept a responsibility for groups within the congregation—visiting them, getting them to come together for prayer and Bible study, embarking on ministries with them for the local church. We could expect similar effects when Anglican churchwardens and readers, Baptist deacons, and Methodist class leaders and lay preachers are touched by the Holy Spirit.

In a number of parishes in the Church of England an eldership has been instituted as a means of recognising charismatic leaders within the congregation. In St. Cuthbert's, York, the elders form a team with responsibilities for the care of certain members, especially within house groups. In St. John's, Harborne, Birmingham, the readers and members of the parochial church council were invited to form an eldership and met weekly for a year to pray about the exercise of this ministry.

For discerning potential lay leadership or elders of this kind, three tests should be applied:

(1) Candidates should be convinced that God is calling them to a share in the pastoral leadership of the local church. It need hardly be said that this does not mean such leadership is for those who are ambitious, seeking a personal status in a congregation. The desire to lead should be part of a greater desire to serve fellow Christians for the sake of Jesus Christ. It is quite likely that such individuals will only become aware of this desire after others have begun to turn to them as leaders and the suggestion is made that they should take initiatives on behalf of the congregation or a group within it.

(2) They should be acceptable to those among whom they will exercise this shared pastoral leadership. This acceptability will have to be assessed from time to time. In modern society the membership of a congregation and its groups changes fairly rapidly in the course of several years, and those who were accepted as leaders in one "generation" are not necessarily the same as those who will be accepted in the next.

(3) They should be acceptable to the rest of the pastoral leadership, especially the clergy. Since the pastor presides over the pastoral leadership team and shares his responsibilities with them, the importance of this is obvious. It means that the leadership team must be totally loyal to the pastor. In some parishes elders enter a simple covenant with their pastor, agreeing to submit to a rule of life which lays out certain objectives in giving their time, their money, their possessions and their abilities to the local church as an expression of their commitment.

All leadership must mirror the principle laid down by Christ: "Whoever would be first among you must be the slave of all. For the Son of Man also came not to be served but to serve, and to give his life as a ransom for many" (Mark 10.44–45).

The pastoral leadership team in the congregation shares with the ordained pastor the responsibility of maintaining unity among the members. Wherever any fresh initiative is taken, that team should be represented in it. Take, for example, the group of young people in the church referred to at the beginning of this chapter. When that group began to emerge in the congregation, the pastoral leadership team should have either delegated one or two of their number to concern themselves with it, or embraced into their team the leader of the group himself. It is difficult to predict what the outcome would have been, but I suspect the group would not have broken away from the congregation so bitterly. It might well have happened then that the charismatic renewal they were experiencing among themselves could have been shared with the rest of the church.

This brings us back to the matter of the relationship between a small group and the congregation to which its members belong. This is nearly always an area that creates problems at some time or other. The one I have described illustrates the problem in its most extreme form. The solution is nearly always to be found in relating the leadership of the group to the pastoral leadership of the congregation. Generally speaking, if this relationship is good, most problems will be solved; if it is bad, they will usually get worse. It is essential that leaders of all kinds in a local church should learn how to work as a team under the pastor's presidency. The leader in the small group—who is becoming a kind of mini-shepherd—finds that from time to time he needs the support of the pastoral leadership team in ministering to his group; the pastoral leadership team also needs his support in ministering to the whole congregation, including his group.

As the pastoral team grows, the role of the ordained leader begins to change. He has to learn to relinquish his immediate pastoral responsibility for individuals in the congregation as they begin to look to other leaders. This is not easy for some pastors—especially when they are temperamentally possessive towards the members of their flock, or when they see the care exercised less adequately because of the lay leader's lack of experience. To be a pastor in a local church where a leadership team is just beginning to grow is rather like standing under a net into which fishes are being thrown—you wonder how many are going to slip through the holes and if you'll be smart enough to catch them! But there are many advantages. Through the leadership team the pastor keeps in touch with a far greater number of people than it was possible for him to do alone. He sees his own lack of skills in certain areas more than adequately supplemented from the charisms of others. He sees new initiatives and new ministries emerging which he could never have contemplated by himself. And, above all, the personal loneliness that many pastors feel when they have to shoulder much of the responsibility for leadership in a local church vanishes as the team begin to gather round him to share his burden.

In fact the pastor finds himself spending less time with individual members of the congregation and more with the team. This is necessary, for if the team are going to serve the local church effectively, they must meet together regularly for prayer, discussion, planning and sharing as well as for social occasions. In a Baptist church the pastor and his team meet together once a month for three to four hours. They begin with a meal (most of the team come to this straight from their places of employment) and then spend the rest of the evening together. Once a year they go away together for a long weekend. At the time I visited them there were over twenty in the team. The effectiveness of that congregation as a witnessing and ministering body was something that was known throughout the town and the surrounding district.

Earlier I suggested that a sign of spiritual renewal in a congregation was an increasing willingness by its members to submit in the Lord to the pastoral leadership. I want to balance this statement now by adding that a sign of spiritual renewal in a pastor is an increasing willingness on his part to submit in the Lord to his congregation. When God begins to call out from among them other leaders, like the mini-shepherds among the groups, then the pastor has to learn how to let that development take place without smothering it at birth. That is the form the pastor's submission often takes.

Great care is needed, however. It is my impression that this new leadership of mini-shepherds is not always to be found among the first individuals who are baptised in the Holy Spirit within a congregation. Sometimes the first leader of a prayer group is one who has not yet been healed of his or her own personal problems in such a way that he or she can minister in a leadership role for others. The three tests described above must be applied discerningly.

The pattern of pastoral care in the congregation changes. Formerly it was pyramidical, with the ordained clergyman at the apex of the pyramid and the congregation spread out under him, all looking to him as the summit and source of spiritual ministry. The new pattern is not pyramidical but cellular. Each group now becomes a cell within the local church with its own mini-shepherd, the leaders all relating to one another under the presidency of the pastor. Research has shown that in many parts of contemporary society, this is the pattern which is most likely to promote Church growth, because it is the pattern within which the every-member ministry is most likely to develop.

7

Congregational Life

"You will know them by what they do," is the *Good News Bible*'s refreshingly direct version of Matthew 7.16 ("You will know them by their fruits.") "The Spirit produces love, joy, peace, patience, kindness, goodness, faithfulness, humility, and self-control," is the same translation's version of Galatians 5.22 ("The fruit of the Spirit . . ."). Although verses like these are quoted over and over again at charismatic meetings, in choruses as well as in addresses, the impression still hangs around that the sign of the Holy Spirit in our lives is in a manifestation of one of the gifts rather than in our attitude towards and relationships with other people. The fascination with charisms such as tongues and healings blurs the basic issue: to be baptised in the Spirit is to be immersed more deeply in the love of God. When a Christian is baptised in the Spirit, then, the first people who should notice this are the members of his own family. If he is not known as a more loving person by them, he should question very seriously the reality of what he has experienced.

I was once discussing the power of God in people's lives with a group of students who were at an enquirer's stage in their approach to the Christian faith. One of them, a girl, said that she was beginning to believe in God because of something that was happening in her family. During the previous few months she had witnessed a remarkable change in her parents. Their attitudes towards one another and towards their daughter had become more loving—more tolerant, more understanding, less critical, less temperamental. The change had begun, she said, after they had started attending a prayer group regularly. The difference it had made in their lives and in the atmosphere of their home was so marked that she could only account for it in terms of God's grace.

By "family" I mean not only a husband with his wife and

children but also any intimate circle of relatives and/or friends. It could be a religious community. A Roman Catholic nun asked me to pray with her for release in the Holy Spirit after I had addressed a public meeting at which she had been present. She confessed that she had irrationally opposed the charismatic movement when she had first heard about it, but the effect of its teachings and practices on some other members of her community had deeply impressed her. They had said nothing to her about their experiences, but she knew they went to a charismatic prayer group. Jesus seemed to be more real for them than before, she noticed; there was an expectancy and joy in all they undertook that had not been there when she first knew them. It was this that had intrigued her and brought her to the meeting in spite of her earlier misgivings. (To complete the story, I should perhaps add that another member of her community and I did pray for her and she opened herself to God in a new way.)

I'm not suggesting, of course, that the other members of the family will always react lovingly towards an individual member's experience of God's love. Sometimes even a Christian household will misunderstand what is happening and accuse the individual of "becoming too religious" or "going all spiritual". Reactions can be more bitter than that. Several young people have told me pathetic tales of how they encountered hostility from their parents because Jesus Christ became more real to them; others have had similar difficulties with husbands, wives, children, relatives and friends. The way of renewal is rarely smooth. Jesus Christ warned us that our foes might be those of our own household—and where baptism in the Spirit is concerned such foes may occasionally be Christians with whom we live. Thus does the devil seek to twist the unifying love of God. Yet it is remarkable how an attitude of loving submission can, with patience, reverse the situation. If we submit to this sort of opposition within our families and refuse to quarrel, the Lord is able to win victories over the enemy in our midst. The apostle's note that "husbands . . . may be won without a word by the behaviour of their wives" (I Peter 3.1) is true of other relationships in a family, too.

One of the things the Lord is showing us these days is the right kind of submission among Christians to one another in groups and congregations as well as in families. Submission is not a popular concept in modern times. The revolt against most forms of authority that is a characteristic of our society is evident in the Church as well. Jesus Christ's injunction that we should serve one another is interpreted almost exclusively in terms of caring for material and personal wants, never in terms of submitting to the other as a brother or sister in the Lord. Many would reject such a suggestion as opening the door to childish dependence, inequality, and perhaps spiritual dictatorship. Indeed, freedom is mistakenly interpreted as liberation from any kind of submission except to Christ himself—a submission which, by its very nature, can mean anything or nothing according to the inclinations of the person concerned.

Submission to a fellow-Christian is a willing and free acceptance of God's order for his people. It is one of the ways in which we die to self. We have already noted that submission to the pastoral leadership is one of the signs of spiritual renewal in a congregation. The submission of members to one another is a further sign. And for the same reason. We do not submit to a fellow-Christian for what he is in himself but for what the Lord does through him by the power of the Holy Spirit. If an individual has a certain charism for a particular ministry in the Church, then others, having discerned and tested that gift, express their obedience to God by submitting to that individual's ministry. For example, it can happen that one member of a congregation has a known gift for—let us say—the discernment of spirits and the ministry of deliverance. When a particular need for this ministry arises, the rest of the congregation or the group should be willing to submit to that member's leadership in the exercise of this ministry. Similarly in a family. The submission of a wife to her husband, or a husband to his wife, or father, mother, child, relative to one another, in the matters that are rightfully their responsibilities in the life of the family, bring healing and enrichment to their relationships. Through submission a beginning is made in the establishment of God's order in the family as well as in the local church.

That beginning is rooted in repentance, when we recognise the weaknesses and failings in our relationships with one another and allow the Holy Spirit to purify and strengthen them. Tensions rise when pride prevents us from acknowledging that anything is wrong, when selfishness overrides our consideration for others. These things have to be healed if God's blessing on us is not to be taken away. Tragically, the personal release which an experience of God's love brings can be abused. It can become a surrender, not to the Spirit of God, but to the world, the flesh and the devil. Family relationships have been destroyed because an individual member has felt free of the restraints that are necessary to enable people to live together. The parents of a young man of twenty recounted how, after an experience that he claimed was baptism in the Spirit, their son became bitterly critical of them, accusing them of lukewarmness in their Christian faith, and eventually leaving home. The suppressed revolt of the teenager had suddenly burst forth following the spiritual release and flooded him, not with love, but with anger towards his parents.

Unless the homes of Christians are being submitted to Jesus Christ, it is unlikely that their local churches will be fellowships warm with his love. It can be quite the reverse. Too often involvement in the activities of a congregation can weaken a family's relationships rather than strengthen them. It is not unknown to find some unhappy husband or wife using the local church as a means of escaping from their responsibilities in the home. Men use the local church and its affairs as a means of getting out of the house where demands are made on them as fathers. Women whose children have grown up and whose husbands are absorbed in their professions join a congregation as a respectable way of occupying their time. Couples with anxieties about their children neglect them for committees, organisations, and meetings associated with the church, telling themselves that they are serving the Lord faithfully outside their homes even if they find it difficult to serve him inside. The same distortions can be found among the unmarried who are too self-centred to become part of an intimate, family-like circle of friends.

The Christian family or group of friends which is experiencing the fruits of spiritual renewal in relationships between its members begins to influence the local church to which it belongs. It is a kind of mini-congregation within the Christian fellowship represented by that local church and thus becomes leaven within the larger lump. This is how the spirituality of a congregation matures. It is not done by campaigns for livelier worship or schemes to involve the laity in church activities; nor is it done by fervent prayer that charismatics can get into positions where they can make friends and influence people! It is done when families and groups within the local church witness to the power of God in their lives by loving one another more. You don't have to talk about renewal in the Holy Spirit when there are people like these in the congregation: you can *feel* it when you are with them, and so do others. It is as if the congregation recognises in that family or in that group a model of what it wants to be in all its relationships—an authentic manifestation of the body of Christ.

It has been my privilege to meet many such families and groups in different denominations: the Anglican churchwarden and his wife who offer their comfortable home in support of people in need (when I knew them they had taken a young couple into their family for a few months following the couple's tragic loss of their first child); the Roman Catholic family whose front-door is always opened to anyone who wants to drop in for a chat and a prayer; the Baptist man and his wife who, believing that the Lord was calling them to establish a community in their house, joined an established community for a year to prepare themselves for the venture; the three young Methodist women who shared their city flat with anyone who was sent their way—a dropout, an alcoholic, a newly-enrolled student without a room. When there is talk of renewal in a local church, these are the people whom I think about first, for it is from such families and groups that the power of God among his chosen is demonstrated.

There is, of course, nothing novel about this. Throughout the history of the Church there have always been families, households, groups and communities whose corporate life has been an example and an encouragement to the local congregation. The households of Stephanas in Corinth and of Aquila and Prisca in Ephesus seem to have been wellknown among Paul's correspondents. At their best the traditional religious communities fulfilled a similar role in the middle ages. In the Church of England the family in the parsonage has been regarded as a model for the rest of the parish (the most famous example being the household of Nicholas Ferrar at Little Gidding, Northamptonshire, in the seventeenth century). Nowadays we do not single out one particular home: the members of every family in a congregation have the opportunity to receive the Spirit of peace and love into their homes and so initiate the process of renewal.

But what then? Suppose certain families and groups in a congregation are being more open to the love of God, what other indications may we look for in the local church and its activities?

One sign of a growing spiritual maturity will be a more expectant attitude towards acts of corporate prayer. This will be noticed not only during church services but also in the prayers that are offered at other times. Take the preliminary prayers that are said by the pastor or the chairman of a church committee before a business meeting. Generally these are regarded as a token of respect to Almighty God rather than a focussing of attention on him. They are like the graces said before a formal meal by the host—they are said because everybody expects them to be said, and once they are over those present feel that they can get on with the real purpose of the meeting. With a movement of charismatic renewal in a congregation, this attitude changes. Prayer is then no longer a preliminary to the agenda; it moves to the centre of the meeting's concern.

The change indicates that for an increasing number of people in that local church, Christ's presence has become more real and therefore prayer has become more worthwhile. Growing faith in a God who speaks to them and acts through them encourages them to bring him into the centre of their thinking rather than leave him on the perimeter. "In everything by prayer and supplication with thanksgiving let your requests be made known to God" (Philippians 4.6). *Everything.* Prayer is no longer restricted to formal services: it pervades the congregation's life.

They trust in God's leading and provision in the things they undertake. Local churches glimpsed the results of such trust when they embarked on stewardship campaigns. Spiritual renewal reveals more. Accepting the fact that God will speak to them and act through them, they look to him for guidance in their life and mission. This is a feature of the Church's attitude in New Testament times which is notably absent today. Nowadays congregations arrange their programmes according to the traditions of their denomination, the customs of the neighbourhood, and their normal annual routine. If anything new is suggested, a decision is made and then afterwards prayers are offered for God's blessing on it. We think we are doing things *for* God when we should be doing things *with* him. In contrast, the Acts of the Apostles and the epistles are full of references which indicate that the early Christians were conscious the Lord worked with them and confirmed the work by the signs that attended it. The charismatic renewal is helping us to recover this sense of Christ's presence and leading.

The gift of prophecy is highly relevant here. As exercised in charismatic circles, this charism has not yet demonstrated its mighty potential. Most of the prophecies I have heard have been words of comfort to individuals facing particular problems. The prophetic utterance to a congregation seeking God's will in their neighbourhood is still rare. But it is obviously a gift of incalculable value to a local church if it is encouraged, tested and acted upon in faith. No charism can make people more aware of the immediacy of God's Word. Fortunately an increasing number of congregations are slowly beginning to seek God's will in this way.

In a Church of England parish a number of prophecies and inspired pictures about the congregation's lifestyle and activities were given during prayer groups and the substance of them was carefully noted down. These notes were duplicated and distributed among the members so that they could discuss them and pray about them. Encouraged by these, the vicar and the congregation reached decisions. Their first venture of faith was in the building of a new church centre. Although funds were low when they started, they received donations on a scale they had never experienced before. From then onwards various new projects in ministry and mission were undertaken, including the establishment of an eldership to share in the pastoral care of the parish with the vicar, and various prophetic utterances played a major role in the shaping and timing of these developments. What is noteworthy about this story is the way in which the prophecies were tested. Groups that follow up things that are said in prophecy without thorough discernment expose themselves to all kinds of dangerous deceptions. The duplicated notes made it possible for this congregation to test everything and to arrive at decisions only after proper consideration. Someone said the notes were special minutes—of a meeting with the Lord!

Another sign of growing maturity is a change in the quality of a congregation's fellowship. In most local churches members can be sociable and hospitable, generous and helpful. But that kind of fellowship is not very different from what we would find in a well-run club. When a congregation begins to walk in the Holy Spirit more faithfully, a quality comes into their relationships that is noticeable to the outsider. He knows these people "have something" that other gatherings lack.

It isn't excessive God-talk; it isn't pious churchianity. It doesn't stifle their differences and their weaknesses, and it doesn't shield individuals from making mistakes. The members of such congregations are, if anything, *more* obviously human than before because they are confident enough to be themselves—they shed that veneer of affability that can so often hide the true character of a person who moves in church circles. Among maturing Christians you feel you are in contact with full-blooded men and women—but people whose lives are being transformed by the Lord in spite of their temptations and sins. You notice a forgiveness among them and a mutual acceptance that gradually distils into a manifestation of divine love.

There is a New Testament word that is not quoted much among Christians but which is nevertheless an important one for any congregation seeking renewal in the Spirit. It is *philadelphia*, the love of the brothers. Paul uses it in Romans 12.10 at the end of a list of charisms: "Love one another with brotherly affection." (It is interesting to note, in passing, how he leads in this epistle from his list of spiritual gifts to an exhortation for mutual love, just as he leads from his list of charisms and ministries in I Corinthians 12 to his hymn of love in chapter thirteen.) *Philadelphia* does not refer to the love of mankind in general but to love between members of the Christian brotherhood. In this relationship love becomes a caricature of itself if any taint of hypocrisy is present: hence it should always be sincere ("Having purified your souls by your obedience to the truth for a sincere love of the brethren, love one another earnestly from the heart"—I Peter 1.22). The word embraces that warm sense of being brothers which bound Christians together in the apostolic age and excited the admiration of pagans. The company of the redeemed are not bound together by ties of kinship and family but by being united to Jesus Christ and to one another in the Spirit. Local churches in renewal are marked by this brotherly love, by a willingness among members to be with one another and to enjoy one another's presence.

Some react against drawing too sharp a distinction between the quality of relationships within a congregation and those within other gatherings of well-intentioned, good-living people. They would argue that Jesus Christ is present even among those who are not consciously his disciples. I have known clergy who have said that they found a more truly Christian spirit outside their congregations than inside them. I would not wish to deny that Christ may be present in non-Christian groupings. The wind of the Spirit blows in different and unexpected places. The Lord is not restricted by the limitations of his people, and there is a hidden presence of God in societies outside the Christian family. Nevertheless, when the Holy Spirit touches a congregation, a brotherly love begins to be experienced among its members that is unlike any other gathering to which they belong. It leads them to regard the congregation as their spiritual home in the fullest sense. Many will move their dwelling-place to be near the local church. Others will refuse offers of promotion and better jobs in order to avoid leaving their congregation. Membership of the body of Christ has become more than a nice concept for sermons: it has become an experienced reality in people's lives.

A third sign of spiritual growth is a deepening concern for people outside the fellowship of the congregation. Christians realise a responsibility for the world because in their Lord they are incorporated into one who is not only creator and redeemer but also consummator of all that exists—"God has made known to us in all wisdom and insight the mystery of his will, according to his purpose which he set forth in Christ, as a plan for the fullness of time, to unite all things in him, things in heaven and things on earth" (Ephesians 1.9–10). It is a concern especially for the oppressed, the underprivileged and the sick, but in modern society it is also a concern for those structures and institutions which control the way we live. A local church which is growing in the Spirit will therefore be involved in its neighbourhood in those matters which affect the livelihood of the people there.

This involvement will not be so intense that it affects the strength of the church's own fellowship. There is much loose talk nowadays about "congregations being turned in on themselves" and "Christian ghettoes". We have to accept that if a group of Christians are going to commit themselves to one another in the Lord, then they will have to spend a fair amount of time with each other and they will have to be interested in one another's affairs. The solidarity of a community is not built up just by sharing a common vision. You need to share your lives with the others, too. But out of that common life individuals and groups will be encouraged and strengthened to concern themselves in what is happening around them. It is an application of the sound military principle that if a regiment is going to fight victoriously, its base must be secure and its lines of communication kept open.

Also, involvement will not be so concentrated that it obscures the Christian belief that ultimately God's kingdom is not of this world. Here and there within the society in which we live we shall discern the marks of that kingdom. The proclamation of the Gospel of God is the announcement that the kingdom is at hand. The kingdom of God is in the midst of his people when they respond in obedience to his Word. But the fulfilment of God's kingdom is beyond this world and Christians can never forget that. When we volunteer for a caring scheme for the elderly because we believe this is the way God is calling us to serve those in need, or when we join a political party because we believe that this is the way the Lord is leading us to right some of the injustices in our society, we shall do so with one eye on God's purposes at the end of time. Christian involvement through the local congregation in the neighbourhood will be penetrated with an other-worldliness that influences their attitude towards plans and activities. That will help its members to remember God's ultimate objectives for them and for his creation.

We can now shape an answer to the question that was modified in an earlier chapter: How does the Lord renew a congregation? Without daring to suggest that we can foresee all that God can do, we can discern a pattern in the way a local church is renewed by his Spirit to give glory to Jesus Christ. The Lord begins with individuals who, as they are more loving in their response to him, become more loving towards those around them—their families, their friends, their groups in the congregation. This love then ripples out to affect others, who recognise in the changed attitudes the work of God. The progress of this ripple can be traced in changes in the congregation, in the quality of their prayer, in the reality of their fellowship, and in their greater concern for others outside their membership. Quite often the congregation becomes cellular in its structure, with small groups forming under elders or lay leaders. The new spirit is sensed by the strangers among them. The activities of the congregation are enriched by a widespread awareness of the presence of God.

Gradually other things in the congregation's life also begin to be transformed—its worship, its mission, its healing ministry, its preparation of new members for initiation, its relationships with congregations of other denominations, with house churches, and with communities. What happens in the local church also begins to affect the wider fellowship of which it is a part. All these we shall now discuss in the following chapters. But to demonstrate that the essence of renewal is not so much a matter of churchgoers doing different things as having greater faith in what they already are by the grace of God, I want to make two qualifications to what I have said in this chapter about the emergence of small groups as an important factor in the development of an every-member ministry.

First, within many existing congregations there are other associations which provide a form of fellowship for those who, for a variety of reasons, are not able to commit themselves to the intimacy of a prayer group such as I have described. Women's meetings and men's clubs attached to the local church may not provide the same dynamic as the prayer group, but nevertheless it should be recognised that these associations can develop into communities where prayer for one another and a ministry of support and healing can be exercised. Many of the organisations that make up the weekday programmes of local churches were originally instituted to provide a ministry among members and others in the neighbourhood apart from the Sunday services, and we should not discount them as a means through which the Spirit can build up the fellowship of the congregation. Spiritual renewal does not mean that a local church abolishes all other forms of coming together except the prayer group!

Second, there will probably always be in most congregations some who are not helped by the small group. Sometimes it may be because of a psychological factor which prevents them from entering into such an intimacy with others easily. Sometimes it may be the objections of a husband or a wife who does not want their partner to be so involved with others. Sometimes it may be that the individual has a more eremitic type of spirituality which reaches up to the Lord in a state of detachment from other Christians. Whatever the reason, their attitude has to be respected, and no attempt should be made to coerce them into a group. Their gifts are of a different kind, and the focus of their commitment to God is in the Sunday worship of the local church without an additional coming together in smaller gatherings.

8

Worship (i)

The worship of a congregation is both an expression and an inspiration of its corporate life. It is an expression of its corporate life because what people do and say when they assemble in church will be influenced by what they believe it means for them to be members of the body of Christ; it is an inspiration because what they do and say will encourage them to manifest the love of God in their daily encounters with others. "Go in peace and serve the Lord," is the form of dismissal found at the end of modern rites. We can only do this if the service we have attended has been an act of spiritual renewal for us.

It is not surprising, therefore, that the influence of the charismatic movement in a local church is often most marked in its worship. Pentecostalism leads us to appreciate more than before what it is to be a fellowship of the Holy Spirit and to rely more confidently on the continuing presence and power of Jesus Christ in our midst. If we respond to the Lord joyfully in our hearts, then this will have its effect on the services we share in. What we do in our charismatic prayer groups and meetings will begin to flow over into our formal Sunday liturgies. There will be pressure to let the spontaneous burst through the traditional structures. Praise will begin to spread out through hymns, psalms, canticles and choruses until it fills the gaps left between other parts of the service. Hands will be lifted in the air and individuals will be carried away in prayers that cannot be confined to the printed texts. What is to be done to preserve unity in a congregation where many want to retain what is familiar to them and who resent these intrusions? In this chapter I will sketch out a few general principles to assist in this process, and in the next chapter illustrate these principles from what I have experienced in local churches as a leader of worship, a member of a congregation, or a guest.

Renewal in the liturgy did not begin with the charismatic movement. Long before Christians had heard of the new Pentecostalism the Holy Spirit had been gently guiding the denominations towards more contemporary forms of worship. Between the two world wars there developed in all the Churches a widespread concern that liturgy should be more relevant and faith-building. The movement for liturgical renewal was backed by careful scholarship so that proposals were seen either as a restoration of ancient simplicity or as a legitimate development of traditions, and gradually those denominations which authorise the forms of worship to be used in their congregations began to change what was said and done when their members attended services. In the last two decades these changes have been considerable. Official texts have been revised, rituals have been simplified, music has been given a more popular flavour, and ecclesiastical buildings have been designed or modified so that they give worshippers a greater awareness of being a gathered community in the midst of whom the Word of God is proclaimed and the sacraments are celebrated. The result has been a veritable revolution. All have been affected—especially Roman Catholics who, in the few years since the Second Vatican Council, have witnessed more changes in their liturgy than their forefathers in the faith had known in a thousand years.

The revolution is not without its critics. Some deplore the disappearance of the old rites for aesthetic or personal reasons. Others complain that modern liturgies have lost the sense of awe and mystery that surrounded the ancient forms. And others are suspicious of the theological presuppositions behind the new texts. Doubtless there is some justification for this opposition, and more work needs to be done. Yet many Christians see in the movement a true impulse of the Holy Spirit, purifying our traditional worship so that it can be a more suitable vehicle through which we may offer to Almighty God our sacrifices of praise and thanksgiving in union with Jesus Christ in modern days.

However, I do not think I am exaggerating when I say that liturgical revision has not always fulfilled the expectations many of us had in it. I was one of those who thankfully welcomed the introduction of the new services in the Church of England. As a vicar in the suburban area known as London-over-the-Border (that part of eastern London which spilled over into the county of

Essex) I had endeavoured to make the *Book of Common Prayer* meaningful to congregations whose educational and cultural background was far removed from those people for whom the old rites had been originally written. The Church of England's *Alternative Services Series Three* seemed more suitable. I spent a good deal of time explaining the meaning of the new services and started using them on Sundays together with modern translations of the Bible. But over a number of years I found—as many other clergy found—that the new forms did not have that transfiguring effect that I hoped for. The congregation appreciated the simplified outline of the rites, the updated language, the sensible lectionary with its thematic presentation of the scriptures, and the rhythm of the modern songs and choruses; they got used to greeting one another in the Peace and they admired the bright colours that were fashionable in ecclesiastical decor. But they did not become a people alive with God's praises.

The new services gave them thrilling acclamations:

> *The Lord is here!*
> *His Spirit is with us!* ...
>
> *Christ has died!*
> *Christ is risen!*
> *Christ will come again!* ...
>
> *Blessing and honour and glory and power*
> *be yours for ever and ever. Amen.*

But I didn't get the sense that they said the words with any burning conviction. They said them because they were printed in the booklet, not because the words clothed with language their personal, inner experience of God in their lives.

I hope I'm not being unfair. I'm sure people in that and similar congregations did believe what they were saying, and I know that there were occasions when our services were buoyant with hope and our hearts were lifted up to the Lord with joy. But such moments were rare. They came unexpectedly at times like the eucharist on Easter Day. More often our services were a routine, repeated Sunday by Sunday with only the variations that the calendar and the lectionary provided and, now and then, some local addition to introduce fresh inspiration. The liturgy seemed far removed from that worship in spirit and in truth that Jesus

Christ spoke of to the woman at the well in Samaria. I could console myself with the thought that the Holy Spirit was there with us in our services, no matter how bored or depressed we felt, for we were gathered together in Christ's name. And I could argue that Sunday services were bound to be something of a routine, anyway, and that the familiar phrases in the liturgy preserved ancient Christian acts of devotion to God. But these explanations were less satisfying after I had begun to experience the Spirit's presence in the worship of a charismatic prayer meeting.

The New Testament teaches us that worship is a manifestation of the Holy Spirit among the people of God. Mary's *Magnificat* sprang from her lips when the Spirit overshadowed her. Zechariah was filled with the Spirit when he sang the *Benedictus*. Simeon's *Nunc dimittis* came from one who had been guided by the Spirit into the temple at the time when the parents brought the child Jesus to it. Christ's own prayer was offered to the Father as he rejoiced in the Spirit. The apostle said that worship was a consequence of being Spirit-filled: "Be filled with the Spirit, addressing one another in psalms and hymns and spiritual songs, singing and making melody to the Lord with all your heart, always and for everything giving thanks in the name of our Lord Jesus Christ to God the Father" (Ephesians 5.18–20). The Church's service of thanksgiving when Peter and John had been released by the Sanhedrin was like a second Pentecost: "And when they had prayed, the place in which they were gathered was shaken; and they were all filled with the Holy Spirit and spoke the word of God with boldness" (Acts 4.31). The vision of heaven's worship received by the author of Revelation happened whilst he was "in the Spirit" (Revelation 4.2).

So the liturgy was to be more than a routine, a correctly executed series of ceremonials and sung or said texts. It was to be our hearts' response to God in obedience to his Spirit. Deep within us there was to be a willing surrender to what was said and done, whether formal or spontaneous. I can sing a hymn joyfully because the tune is a favourite of mine—but that is not the true inspiration of worship. I can admire the sound of the words of a traditional prayer as I recite them with the rest of the congregation—but that is not praying. The singing of the hymn and the saying of the prayer only become worship when they express something that I know is real either in my experience of the Lord's love or in my acceptance of his promises. That was the lesson the charismatic movement taught me—bringing to the front of my consciousness something that I had been intellectually aware of before but that had never conjoined vitally with anything I had experienced.

Not that I always feel like this when I go to church! Our wayward emotions are not tamed by baptism in the Spirit; they have to be disciplined each day. But if we are learning to walk in the Spirit then we shall also be learning to crucify the flesh with its passions and desires. Beneath our discontents and rebellions there will be an underlying inclination to participate in the worship of God's people, even when the liturgy is not all that we think it should be. It is this change in our attitude towards worship that is a characteristic of spiritual renewal: we come to a service with a lively expectancy that we shall meet the Lord. I know I have sometimes gone to church on a Sunday morning with a depressed feeling. I have told myself that it was going to be a dull affair—the same old prayers, the same old hymns. But when the service began I have set my feelings and thoughts on one side and asked God to rekindle in me the fire of his love. Perhaps I have prayed quietly in tongues for a few moments, or imagined him standing in the midst of his people. Then a transformation has taken place. The old hymns have spoken of God's mighty works, and the old prayers have given me fitting words with which to vocalise my response. Even the most casual sermon has contained a thought or an encouragement from the Lord for me. The liturgy has become what it is meant to be—a proclamation of God's word and a renewing of his grace.

This is why the technical process of liturgical revision is generally of secondary importance for many charismatics. On the whole they prefer the new services because they regard them as more suitable vehicles for worship today, but revision is not essential. The Holy Spirit who guided the compilers of older rites, such as those in the *Book of Common Prayer*, is the same now as he was then, and the Spirit in us moves in harmony with the inspired texts from the past. For the same reason charismatics have very ecumenical tastes in liturgy. When they share in the worship of other denominations, they are less concerned to mark down the differences between that worship and their own; they are more appreciative of the way the Holy Spirit has led that particular tradition to respond to God's Word in its liturgy.

When we discern the Spirit's guiding in our worship, the distinction between formal and spontaneous worship is less important. What matters is that every tongue should confess that Jesus Christ is Lord, to the glory of God the Father. The fixed, authorised texts have their invaluable purposes. They safeguard us from the whims of individual leaders. They enshrine scriptural truths in our response to God. They preserve for us gems from the Church's treasury of devotion. But they are not intended to displace completely the free expression of any individual group or congregation. As a result of the liturgical renewal, the new services recognise the need for free expressions and provide opportunities for them. This is what liturgists call "creativity in worship". To borrow a rough analogy from the concert hall, modern rites are like musical scores: they present us with a pattern of notes created by one gifted to make music but we—the orchestra—have to interpret those scores in performance in our own way, with improvisations and experiments, under the baton of the Spirit!

All forms of liturgy contain the four elements that we noted in an earlier chapter. Whether we are at a eucharist, an evening service, a baptism, a confirmation, a harvest festival, or a marriage, there will be an introduction, a ministry of the Word of God, a response by the people, and a dismissal. Spontaneous contributions—a prayer, an act of praise, a Pentecostal charism, a testimony, a reading, a song—can be related to one or more of these elements in the way I described when discussing leadership in a charismatic prayer meeting. Then such contributions will either enable us to hear the Word of God more clearly or encourage us to respond to him with greater faith and obedience. Creativity in worship brings the congregation into a more vivid awareness that God is with them, speaking, comforting, healing, guiding, equipping. It also rescues its members from that over-dependence upon the fixed text that stunts their personal growth in the life of prayer. Anglicans and Roman Catholics especially are often tongue-tied outside the familiar fixed forms. But once they are released from this, their grounding in the traditional liturgies of their denominations provides a sure foundation on which their own expressions of thanksgiving and praise can be built.

When a congregation is submissive to the Holy Spirit, what is formal and what is spontaneous in its worship merges into a lovely unity. I have frequently heard praises and petitions of great beauty come from the lips of inspired individuals who have little academic knowledge of the traditions of liturgical devotion. I have heard them take up ideas and phrases from the scripture readings or from the liturgical texts and use them as a basis for acts of devotion that embraced the thoughts of everyone in the church. If what they said could have been written down it would be worthy of instant publication along with the prayers of such authors as Michel Quoist or Rex Chapman. I have seen individuals or groups move from their seats into a spontaneous dance or a gesture of fellowship that was entirely unselfconscious because it was an offering of their bodies in worship to the immediate inspiration of the Holy Spirit.

Those Christians who have been accustomed only to free worship often find in the formal texts material that they want to make their own. For example, they are usually familiar with the scriptural pattern in which prayer is offered to God the Father in thanksgiving for all that Jesus Christ has done which is now available for us through the Holy Spirit. When they read the traditional ascription to the Holy Trinity that ends the ancient collects and prayers, they immediately recognise the same inspiration that has moved them (it is a pity that our contemporary liturgists have not yet restored the oldest form of this ascription: "Glory be to the Father through Jesus Christ in the Holy Spirit").

A Pentecostal minister, living with relatives during a period of enforced unemployment, worshipped each Sunday for several months in a rather traditional Anglican church which had not moved very far in liturgical reform. "I hated it at first," he told me, "because I've never used a printed prayer in my life. But the Lord had a work to do in me. He showed me how he can be glorified in the most formal kind of prayers—and I love them now!" I reminded him that the worship of heaven appeared to be very formal indeed according to the Book of Revelation!

Achieving a balance between what the Spirit gives us through the formal and what he provides through the spontaneous for our worship only comes to a congregation and its leader with experience. The first reflects the institutional dimension of the Church, the second the charismatic. Each needs the other. The formal rites, revised from time to time after testing by what God reveals through his Word in the scriptures, expounds in the Church's traditions, and interprets in the light of our experience of him now, provide us with a groundplan on which our acts of worship can be built. The groundplan gives us the assurance that the main elements in that act of worship will be included. The spontaneous, also tested by what God reveals, builds on that groundplan by making us aware of the living presence of Jesus Christ in his worshipping Church and of the need for our personal response to the Father through him in the power of the Holy Spirit. In this way both the formal and the spontaneous are Spirit-gifted—charismatic.

Generally speaking the amount of spontaneity in a congregation has to be less as the numbers grow. A large assembly can do some things freely—sing in the Spirit, join in a variety of hymns and choruses, and take part in processions (if space permits). But it cannot have the same amount of freedom as a small group of a dozen or twenty. Charismatics should remember this when they are critical of the services in their churches for not being as spontaneous as the worship in their prayer groups. A congregation of a hundred or more needs a fixed order of service and the leadership of a pastor as a basis for its worship, and the possibilities of sharing are reduced according to acoustics and visibility. The picture of shared worship preserved in Paul's first letter to the Church in Corinth is sometimes quoted as a model of what a service should be like. Whatever else we can say about the Corinthian congregation, it could not have been a very large one, otherwise it would not have been possible for everyone to be ready "with a psalm or a sermon or a revelation, or ready to use his gift of tongues or to give an interpretation" (chapter 14, verse 26, *Jerusalem Bible*).

There is a widespread assumption that worship has to be more emotional if it is to be more charismatic. This is because charismatic worship is associated with greater demonstrations of freedom than is customary in many Western churches—*Alleluias*, clapping, body-swaying, hands held in the air, and so on. Two comments have to be made about this. First, some charismatic groups have tended to borrow expressions of penitence and devotion from the classical Pentecostal Churches, whose forms of worship have been influenced by the culture of the black American and West Indian peoples who have formed the majority of their membership. To the Western churchgoer, who is likely to come from a white Anglo-Saxon middle-class environment, some of these features appear more emotional and unnecessarily exaggerated. This borrowing is, I believe, only a passing phase. Charismatics are learning to adapt what they are taking over from Pentecostal worship to their own traditions. A parallel might be drawn with the experience of the Anglo-Catholic movement. In the first flush of enthusiasm a century ago, certain Church of England clergy introduced into the worship of their parish churches ritual practices and devotional aids from the Roman Catholicism of southern Latin Europe. Eventually these were dropped when it was realised that few English Christians were helped by them.

Secondly, the worship of the white Anglo-Saxon middle-class Christian is usually highly cerebral. The bride's mother may be permitted to weep at her daughter's wedding, and the baby may be expected to cry at his baptism, but it is accepted that other signs of feeling should be stifled. Consequently emotion is channelled (for in the end feelings cannot be stifled: they must find an outlet somewhere) into other aspects of the service—the music and the singing, the ceremonial and the vestments, the flowers and the decoration. This is why certain churchgoers get upset if the ceremonial is changed or the setting of the hymn is unfamiliar: they have a lot of emotional capital locked away in such things!

Now there may be good reasons why people are fearful about getting too emotional in worship. Leaders can work up the feelings of a congregation artificially so that the service becomes more of an entertainment than a liturgy, and the effect of such demonstrations of emotion on the more susceptible members of a local church has to be considered. But there is surely a place in many congregations for more natural expressions of joy, sorrow, fellowship and compassion than is common. What is required to bring many services alive is that they should be more genuinely *human*, particularly in those denominations which have been wedded to formal worship. More than anything television has exposed the stiff, unreal attitudes of many church dignitaries, liturgical groups (servers, choirs), and congregations when they participate in services. At the great service of thanksgiving in St. Paul's Cathedral for the jubilee of Queen Elizabeth II in 1977, the most heart-warming moments were the glimpses of the members of the royal family shaking hands and chatting in a relaxed way with the clergy in the entrance before the processions moved off. Once the service started, a deathly rigidity seemed to possess both congregation and leaders. No doubt the solemnity of the occasion was oppressive, plus the knowledge that the service was being televised round the world, but it magnified in an appalling way the effects of formal worship on human beings. It has been said that we shrivel as human beings if we do not grow in worship. The words might well be twisted round: worship shrivels if we do not act like liberated human beings whilst we are sharing in it.

In this liberation of man's worship, singing has a vital role to play. But unfortunately the music used in many of our churches has been drawn from a limited field. The argument has been that everything in the liturgy, including the music, should be aesthetically acceptable according to the standards set by those professional musicians whose ideals are measured by the traditions of English cathedrals and churches where there is a trained choir. Only the best is good enough for God, it is said.

The story is told of an American visitor who was taken to a service in the ornate chapel of the Royal Holloway College by the principal. When the choir began to sing an anthem, the American began to join in, only to be "hushed" by his host.

"May I not offer my praises in the house of God?" protested the visitor.

"This is not the house of God!" replied the principal severely. "This is the Royal Holloway College!"

Whether apocryphal or not, the story illustrates the problem. When pastors and members of congregations have attempted to introduce into church services some of the more popular, ephemeral music associated with charismatic prayer meetings, they have encountered the hostility of organists and choirmasters. We have to look together at the concept of what is best in worship. While not wishing to deny the need to educate congregations' tastes in music and to train choirs according to the standards set by the Royal School of Church Music, we have to recognise that, like every other art form, music is the servant of the liturgy, and the purpose of the liturgy is to enable people to hear the Word of God and to respond to that Word in appropriate ways. The task of the expert—the organist, the choir, the soloist, the guitar group, the

sacred dance troupe, the drama players—is to assist a congregation in the liturgy, not to treat them as a captive audience. In
the movement of today's worship, the easily memorised scriptural
chorus may not be worth much aesthetically, but it may be highly
satisfactory at a certain moment in a service as a simple means of
helping a congregation to reflect on the Word of God. A sung
interpretation following a gift of singing in the Spirit may not
qualify for entry into a music competition, but it may at a certain
moment express exactly a congregation's response to the Word of
God more than an anthem which has been practised for weeks
beforehand. Doubtless ninety-nine per cent of the songs of the
charismatic renewal will be forgotten before long, but they are
serving Christians well today. We live in an age when the dis-
posable is as useful as the long-life.

With tact and patience it is possible to widen a congregation's
repertoire beyond the more traditional hymns. Even cathedral
choirs now tackle some of the productions of the Twentieth
Century Light Music Group! Unfortunately there are still a few
church musicians around who fail to see the needs of others
beyond their own presuppositions. On the day this chapter was
being drafted a vicar told me that his choirmaster had walked out
of church the previous Sunday morning because he (the vicar) had
spontaneously invited the congregation to sing a chorus (unac-
companied) as a fitting way of responding to a sermon he had just
preached!

9

Worship (ii)

In trying to illustrate ways in which the charismatic renewal is influencing the worship of congregations, I am conscious of a personal limitation. Almost all my experience of leading church services has been within the Church of England. I have attended the services of other denominations only as a visitor or a preacher. Consequently my knowledge of them is very sketchy. If this chapter seems orientated towards Anglican practices, therefore, I must ask the non-Anglican reader to make allowances for it.

I suggested earlier that the charismatic prayer meeting is, from one point of view, a protest against the kind of worship that many Christians find in their own churches. The spontaneous outpouring of prayer and praise, the manifestations of Pentecostal charisms such as prophecies, tongues and interpretations, the powerful sense of fellowship and the opportunities for personal ministry, are so different from what these Christians are used to that for them the prayer meeting opens up new dimensions of worship before their wondering eyes. They continue to attend the services at their own churches, but for a proportion of them the prayer meeting becomes their "real" worship. The popularity of the prayer meeting, therefore, is a judgement against the tepid support that many churchgoers give to their own services. Not every churchgoer, of course, comes into this category: only those who attend churches where the liturgy is chilly and formal with routine. But the number of churches where the liturgy is like this is not small.

Yet there is another point of view. What we do when we attend a charismatic prayer meeting is fundamentally the same as when we go to church. Both are a *leitourgia*, a service offered by God's people to the Father through Jesus Christ. Both are gifts of corporate prayer and praise in response to God's Word. Even the

most solemn act of worship, the service of Holy Communion, is a
manifestation of the Holy Spirit in Word and sacrament, as the
text of the modern Church of England eucharist demonstrates:

> *Accept our praises, heavenly Father,*
> *through your Son, our Saviour Jesus Christ;*
> *and as we follow his example and obey his command,*
> *grant that by the power of your Spirit*
> *these gifts of bread and wine may be to us*
> *his body and his blood . . .*
>
> *Accept through him, our great high priest,*
> *this our sacrifice of thanks and praise;*
> *and as we eat and drink these holy gifts*
> *in the presence of your divine majesty,*
> *renew us by your Spirit,*
> *inspire us with your love,*
> *and unite us in the body of your Son,*
> *Jesus Christ our Lord.*

Those prayers are powerful invocations of charismatic blessings
on the sacramental signs and on the people who are gathered to
receive them. What the prayer meeting does is to present us with
opportunities to explore the meaning of those invocations. From
this point of view, then, the prayer meeting is more like a school or
a laboratory for worship. In it we can discover some of the
consequences of Pentecostal renewal in the Christian and in the
Church, expressed in forms of corporate worship that cannot
immediately be transposed into the setting of our traditional
liturgy. But because both the church service and the prayer meeting are genuine liturgy, there is an intimate relationship between
them. When we become more sensitive to the Spirit's leading in
the comparative freedom of the prayer meeting, we learn things
that are directly relevant to our experience of worship within the
formal worship of our congregation.

This is an important lesson for most ordinary churchgoers, who
do not have much opportunity to share in acts of worship that are
radically different from what they are used to. An individual may
attend a special service somewhere, or he may look in on an
experimental act of worship on television, but such experiences
are occasional in every sense of the word. They are unrelated to

any personal spiritual awakening and they are, at their best, only interesting events to be remembered but not copied. As we have seen, the charismatic prayer meeting is not like this. What happens there usually has a direct bearing on what participants are realising about the presence of God in their own lives. And some of them have opportunities of contributing to the worship in the meeting in ways that are not available for them in their own church services.

But prayer meetings are even more important for the clergy, especially those who have an opportunity to lead in them. The average pastor is usually only familiar with liturgical leadership in the kind of service that is traditional in his own denomination. There are few openings for him to preside over other types of worship. If he is—like most Anglican clergy—used to leading from a prescribed text, he has little chance to learn the technique of controlling an assembly in which there is much spontaneity. In the prayer meeting he can set aside these restraints. If he is personally being liberated by the Holy Spirit, his new sense of freedom will make him eager to accept those charisms which equip him to lead in the new situation. He is not cramped by the custom of his parish church or the expectations of his Sunday congregation. He can learn how to keep order in the midst of creativity, how to lead the congregation from one stage to the next as they respond to God, how to discern the Pentecostal gifts, how to exercise discipline over those who become self-assertive, and how to sense the movement of the Holy Spirit in the congregation and encourage its expression in appropriate ways. In this learning process he can discover that what comes to him from his tradition is given a fresh relevancy in the midst of what is new.

Gandhi once said: "There go my people, I am their leader, I must follow them." What the denominations with long and revered liturgical traditions have to recognise is that the quest for renewal in worship does not end when they have finally agreed on the most acceptable modern rites. They also have an obligation to follow the Holy Spirit as he leads the people of God to pray together. And as people pray together, they will be guided to expressions and gestures that spring from their own response to the love of God as they experience it in their lives, and these have an authentic place in their worship, integrated with the expressions and gestures that have been handed down to them through their denominations. I want to stress this, for the lesson of the charismatic prayer group is not one of copying but of discerning.

What I mean is this. Those who have only a superficial knowledge of prayer meetings can easily be misled into thinking, "It would be nice to try that out in our church," when they witness for the first time some new thing. It might be a way of praying together, a method of singing, a technique for encouraging participants to minister to one another. But unless that word, that gesture, or that symbol meets the beliefs, hopes or needs of the congregation among whom it is introduced, then it is not true worship; it is a gimmick imposed upon them to satisfy an individual's thirst for novelty. Unfortunately since the liturgical movement began, we have suffered much from enthusiasts who have been fascinated by some item in an experimental act of worship and tried to incorporate it into their own churches, with little thought of what that item was intended to express. It would be a thousand pities if the potential for renewal in worship that is contained within the charismatic prayer meeting, was rejected by large numbers of Christians simply because a few insensitive pastors tried to force congregations into practices that were unrelated to their own spiritual inclinations.

Worship in local churches will become more charismatic when pastors and their congregations become more aware of the living Lord present in their midst by his Spirit and when they seek appropriate ways in which to recognise him. I remember how my own attitude towards church services and my role as a leader of worship began to change after I had experienced the Lord's dynamic presence in prayer meetings. I was brought up in an Anglo-Catholic tradition that regarded one of the most important things about the liturgy was that it should be done "decently and in order". Certain things were traditional and tasteful and worthy of God: other things weren't. It was my job to uphold the former and banish the latter (though the criteria for deciding this were decidedly limited). I believed that if the Holy Spirit manifested himself to us as we worshipped, it was because we were doing everything according to the directions laid down in the liturgical manual in fashion at the time. So everybody who participated in the service—servers, organist, choir, readers, sidesmen—had to be drilled until they played their part correctly. If the reader stumbled over a difficult word, or the sidesman started taking the collection during the wrong hymn, this spoilt the worship. It had not been a "good service".

The change in me began when I sensed a new freedom in worship, both as a participant and as a leader. I was less concerned about saying and doing what I thought was correct according to the manuals. I was more eager to obey the Holy Spirit's promptings as we moved through the service. I looked more at God and less at the people around me. When I presided over a service in the parish church, I saw myself as the congregation's servant, set among them by the Lord to help them to respond to him. What mattered was that I should help them to say and do what they felt they wanted to say and do as they opened themselves to the Holy Spirit. The essential spiritual gift in that ministry was not an encyclopaedic knowledge of ritual but discernment and sensitivity. "You've changed!" a member of the congregation said to me after the service one morning. By the tone of her voice I knew she was half-approving and half-disapproving—but I felt the approving part in her came from God!

This was the chief influence the charismatic renewal had on me. The other influences were secondary. For example, when I first attended prayer meetings in London sponsored by the Fountain Trust in the 'sixties, I was interested in the effect the introductory chorus-singing had on people as they entered the hall. I was also attracted by the friendly way in which the leader made people feel at home by a few casual remarks at the beginning of the meeting. To an Anglican like myself this was entirely novel. The only introductory music I had ever known before a church service was an organ voluntary, and I had never heard a clergyman make any friendly remarks at the beginning of a service. All I had heard a priest do was to announce the first hymn. When the new cathedral at Coventry was opened, the clergy were criticised for adopting the practice of saying "good morning" or "good evening" before a service. There were letters to the church press in protest!

It was when the liturgical committee of the parish discussed the arrangements for the midnight eucharist on Christmas Eve that the first of these lessons came in useful. Although the service did not begin until eleven-forty-five, people started arriving in church soon after eleven o'clock in order to secure a seat near the front, and chattered among themselves until the service commenced.

The committee argued that this created an undevotional atmosphere in the church. Voices were raised above the organ voluntary and somehow the service seemed to get off to a bad start. It was then that I thought of the introductory chorus-singing at the prayer meeting. Why not sing carols and read lessons for half-an-hour before the midnight eucharist? I suggested. The liturgical committee enthusiastically agreed and we tried it. It was an immediate success. Those who came to church early enjoyed the carol-singing, and those who arrived after it had begun remarked how thrilling it was to walk up the road towards the lighted church at night and to hear the sound of the carols coming from within. It gave them a sense of joy and expectancy in coming to church that they had not known before.

I also began to make a few remarks about the theme of the scripture readings and the purpose of the service before I announced the first hymn. Over a number of weeks I gradually developed this to include other things, like a word of welcome to visitors and a quick congregational choir practice for a new tune. Looking back, these now seem very minor innovations (they must have been done in many other churches long before anyone heard of the charismatic renewal!). But they were the beginnings of a slow relaxation in one Anglican priest and his congregation, bringing in a breath of commonsense humanity into an over-formalised liturgy. By changing a few little things in this way it became possible, in two or three years, to look for more radical changes without causing a major upheaval in the minds of the more conservative members of the church. It is the change in attitudes that matters. When a congregation can learn to discern what is the best way of ordering their worship at a particular time without relying over-much on "what we've always done", then members are willing to try experiments without feeling restless and insecure.

The two minor innovations I have described belong to that element in the liturgy which I have called the *Introduction*. Perhaps this was significant. By relaxing the style of the introduction to the service first, people were able to consider changes in the other parts. Sharing in the ministry of the Word has never been easy in Anglican churches. Preachers are supposed to have been authorised by the diocesan bishop, and the size of many church buildings demands a skill in public speaking that few lay members of a congregation possess. Participation in this ministry has usually been limited to the reading of the scriptures and the preaching of the sermon: the former by a layman or laywoman, the latter by an ordained clergyman or a licensed reader. An anthem or solo that draws out the theme of the readings comes under this heading, involving the choir or a guest singer.

The charismatic renewal has increased our expectations in the ministry of the Word in a number of ways. First, the reading of the scriptures and the preaching of a sermon has been infused with a greater sense of God's presence. In many Anglican and Roman Catholic churches especially, this part of the eucharist was regarded as a preliminary to the focus of the service—the prayer of consecration and the Communion. Through baptism in the Spirit Christians of these and other denominations hear the Lord speaking much more directly to them. The words of the Bible are read with conviction (what a difference it makes when a reader in church *sounds* as if he believes in what he is saying!) and sermons are preached with a faith that God is anointing the preacher for his task. Congregations are learning more about *receiving* sermons—that is, to have that attitude of expectancy that engenders a spiritual dialogue between the man in the pulpit and the people in the pews. As a preacher I can always tell when a congregation are merely listening to me out of politeness and when they are listening as those who hope to hear the Lord through (or in spite of) what I say.

Secondly, prayer meetings are showing us that people in the pews often have something to share in the ministry of the Word, too. They can tell how an incident in their lives during the past week has revealed God's love to them and encouraged them. I use the word "testimony" with some hesitation: these sharings are not the kind of testimonies associated with certain evangelistic campaigns when individuals recount how they have been converted, but rather personal stories of how the Lord helped them in everyday situations and problems. Testimonies like these can be inserted into the Sunday service from time to time. Tom Walker of St. John's, Harborne, Birmingham, has a persuasive way of inviting individuals to the chancel step in his church and interviewing them, helping them to give a testimony through a question-and-answer technique. For those who listen the Gospel often comes alive for them with up-to-date illustrations. Testimonies carefully handled can increase the sense that what a congregation is celebrating in the service is, not only what God did through his Christ in New Testament times, but also what he is doing through him now. Testimonies have the added bonus of encouraging those who make them to be more articulate about their faith.

Thirdly, there is a wider appreciation of what God can say through other media of communication in church—drama, mime, dance, movement, visual aid. This sort of thing is not confined to the worship of congregations that have been touched by the charismatic renewal, of course, but the renewal strengthens the impression that what is performed is to be accepted by both participants and congregation as a gift from God rather than an artistic presentation. These developments have caused unease among some churchgoers who associate dancing and drama with secular entertainment, but if we see within human expressions of communication that which is created by God and which can be consecrated for his service (the basic lesson of the charismatic renewal itself), then these things can enrich the worship of any congregation once they are released and gifted for them.

Fourthly, our understanding of the ministry of the Word has been built up by the Pentecostal charisms of prophecy, speaking in tongues, and interpretations. These spiritual gifts cannot be planned into a service in the same way that a testimony or a new chorus can. They are usually spontaneous—the result of God's anointing at a particular moment. So they cannot be slotted into the liturgy in a tidy way during that section which is called the ministry of the Word in the service books. It is the leader's task to control these manifestations and to help the congregation to test them and to relate them to the rest of that ministry. This requires a high degree of receptivity on the side of the congregation. I have heard prophetic utterances that brought congregations to their knees in penitence or joy, and I have heard other utterances devoid of inspiration that spoke only of the anger and frustration of the one who gave them.

One striking manifestation of a Pentecostal charism took place when I was a visiting preacher one Sunday evening in a small country church in Lancashire. It seemed a very ordinary even-song—psalms sung to simple chants, hymns taken from *Ancient and Modern*, intercessory prayers read devoutly from a book. The congregation was not large—thirty or so—but there was an atmosphere of love among them: I noticed that two people, who were obviously suffering from some form of mental deficiency, appeared to feel quite at home and were accepted without any fuss. The only un-Anglican thing that happened occurred immediately after the intercessory prayers and before the sermon. A woman in the congregation stood up and spoke in tongues. When she had finished there was a long silence. Then a man on the other side of the church gave an interpretation. To my astonishment that interpretation underlined in a fresh way the point I was to make in the sermon that I had prepared but not yet preached! I have rarely experienced a more encouraging send-off when I mounted the steps to the pulpit!

The charismatic renewal is helping us to loosen up in our response to the Word of God in the liturgy so that we are not entirely dependent upon a previously-chosen list of hymns and songs. We are learning to incorporate spontaneous singing into our normal worship, especially singing in the Spirit which provides a congregation with a form of free-wheeling praise. Singing in the Spirit is usually the most acceptable type of Pentecostal prayer in a congregation where some do not speak in tongues. Non-glossolists can be invited to hum tunes or sing choruses quietly: many have on such occasions been given the gift of tongues themselves during the singing. The giving of the Peace goes well in churches where members feel free to act naturally as well as devoutly during worship. Those who have participated in open prayer at meetings find that they can contribute to the intercessions in church. The advantage of having a formal outline of these intercessions, such as is provided in the new eucharistic rites, is that individuals soon learn how to offer their intentions in the appropriate section.

We shall discuss the ministry of prayer for healing later, but it ought to be mentioned here as one of the responses to the Word of God in the liturgy that is welcomed in most congregations, once the purpose of that ministry has been carefully explained. If a few in the congregation have already been present at prayer meetings where this ministry has been exercised, then their participation helps those who initially find it rather strange (particularly those individual Christians who have doubts about whether we should expect God to heal outside the usual medical processes). The need for healing and support in the midst of illnesses is found in every congregation. Intercessions for the sick are common in services. It is not a big step to suggest first that individuals in the congregation should name those for whom prayers are desired, and then to invite people in the congregation to receive the laying on of hands if they require (for example, those who are to be admitted to hospital for treatment during the following week). It does not matter that the Sunday service is not a service of prayer for healing in the narrow sense. Basically *every* service is to invoke the Lord's healing grace into our lives. The ministry of the Word, the form of confession of sin, the prayer for forgiveness, and the affirmation of faith that most formal services include, are sufficient preparation for those who are to participate. How the healing ministry is conducted in a particular service is a matter for local decision. At a eucharist the laying on of hands can be done either during the intercessions for the sick, or after the Communion while the individuals coming for that ministry are still kneeling at the altar rail, or at the end of the service before the dismissal.

In one Church of England parish, prayer with the laying on of hands for healing was introduced about once a month after the main Sunday eucharist. It was the custom for coffee to be served in church after the service and the vicar simply announced that those who wished to be prayed for should remain behind after the others had gone home. He only had to do this once or twice before the congregation unanimously asked him to incorporate the ministry within the eucharist itself.

Whatever we consider introducing into our normal Sunday services, we must take into account the physical limitations imposed on us by the size of the congregation and the type of building in which they meet, as well as the ideas and prejudices of the individuals who make up the congregation. A church building with fixed pews cannot be used as flexibly as a hall with movable chairs. A technique from the *Come Together* service—already described, when a congregation is subdivided into groups of three or four people to pray among themselves for ten minutes or so—becomes less effective if used every week. It is unrealistic to expect the same kind of intimacy in the intercessions of a congregation of one-hundred-and-fifty as in a prayer group of ten. Furthermore, no congregation coming together regularly week after week can avoid the patterns imposed by a routine. It is the task of the formal liturgy to enable a congregation to accept a disciplined orderliness and at the same time find a freedom within the routine for its own creativity. The Church's liturgical calendar with its festivals and seasons provides an annual rhythm of variations, leading the congregation through the lectionary to reflect on the great saving acts of God from creation to the Second Advent. Faithfully used, this variation can be the inspiration of much spontaneous and local offering in worship by individuals and groups in the local church.

What about the charismatic prayer meeting itself? If it is a school or laboratory for liturgy, does this mean it will eventually disappear as its lessons are applied to the regular worship of the local church? It is difficult to foretell what its future will be. Although it might soon outlive its usefulness as a focus for experimental worship, it has other functions as well. Where it draws together Christians of different denominations, it provides an opportunity for ecumenical worship in a form that has not been readily accessible before. In some local churches it offers an occasion when the congregation and people who meet in house groups can come together on a monthly or bi-monthly basis for a more leisurely and free time of worship and fellowship than is possible on Sunday mornings or evenings. In other places it can act as an additional service for people who, for various reasons, are not able to attend the Sunday worship of a congregation. And as long as there are Christians in the local churches who seek further instruction on the charismatic renewal, it will continue as a means of teaching about the experience of the Pentecostal charisms in a setting of prayer and praise. It could be that a mid-week meeting of this kind will be in the programme of some congregations for many years to come.

In an earlier chapter I described a prayer meeting I attended in a town in the south of England. I shall end this chapter by describing a eucharist in a Church of England parish to illustrate the influence of the charismatic renewal on the services of an ordinary congregation. It was memorable because it showed me how a particular parish was moving under the Holy Spirit to order its worship with a balance between what is traditional and what is spontaneous. The parish had been influenced by the renewal for about two years. I want to emphasise that what happened on that occasion is not necessarily what should happen anywhere else. I repeat—worship becomes more charismatic, not by copying what others do, but by being obedient to the leading of the Holy Spirit in one's own local church.

The service was a sung eucharist to celebrate a patronal festival on a weekday evening. The liturgy was due to begin at 9.30 p.m., but at eight o'clock on that day each week the parish had an open prayer meeting in the church and about twenty or so turned up for that. During the first hour there was chorus-singing, prayer and a talk by me, and at one point the vicar shared with us a particular concern that he had and asked for our prayers about it. By nine o'clock the church—a modern building with a free-standing altar—was fairly full, and the vicar and I slipped away into the sacristy with the four men who were to act as servers to get ready for the eucharist. The singing and praying continued in the church under the leadership of others.

At half-past-nine the sanctuary party (the vicar, the servers and myself, all vested) processed through the church led by a thurifer swinging a censer. The *Series Three Order for Holy Communion* began with a hymn. Silence and a short chorus separated the epistle and the gospel and after the sermon there was another period of silent reflection. This was broken when a member of the congregation shared a word of wisdom illuminating one aspect of the scripture readings that I had not mentioned in my sermon.

The intercessions followed the set form provided in the rite, and the congregation were invited to join in with their own contributions. The fact that people were seated in a semi-circle round the altar made it possible for everyone to hear what someone else was saying, especially as each one who contributed stood up to speak. There was no sense of rush and yet the congregation seemed to impose a discipline on itself by not lingering too long on each section. When we came to the section where prayers are offered for the sick, one person asked for the laying on of hands and three people sitting near her stood up to pray with her.

The giving of the Peace was a joyful confusion. We moved around shaking hands or embracing one another for several minutes. But once the vicar had returned to the altar, there was an instant return to orderliness and we launched into a glorious chorus for the offertory. I was reminded of those plays where periods of solemnity are interrupted by moments of informality, the contrast strengthening the different moods. During the eucharistic prayer the acclamations were shouted with fervour, and at the end of that prayer there was a time of gentle singing in the Spirit in which we were held together in an act of adoration.

The Communion was distributed whilst a group led the congregation in a series of quiet songs. One couple with their two children remained kneeling at the altar after the distribution. The vicar explained that they were leaving the parish the following week to go and live in another part of England. He prayed for them and laid hands on them, invoking the Holy Spirit to strengthen them, to bless them in their new home, and to equip them to share in the life and witness of another congregation. There were tears in a few eyes as the family returned to their chairs. The service ended with a final burst of praise. The sanctuary party did not process formally back to the sacristy. We simply slipped out of our vestments behind the altar and joined the congregation for coffee in the church.

10

Mission

> *Send us out*
> *in the power of your Spirit*
> *to live and work*
> *to your praise and glory.*

The prayer which the congregation says together at the end of the *Series Three Order for Holy Communion* points them from their worship to their mission in the world. Worship renews the Church in her mission. Indeed, worship and mission are not two separate aspects of the Church's life but one. In this characteristic she reflects the life of her Saviour. The work of Jesus is described in the New Testament in terms of both worship and mission. The message of the Gospel is that the Father sends the Son and, in turn, Jesus sends his disciples in the power of the Holy Spirit. Their obedient response to him is their worship in the fullest sense of the word. Christ "loved us and gave himself for us, a fragrant offering and sacrifice to God" (Ephesians 5.2): the mission of Jesus interpreted in cultic imagery. The same imagery is employed by Paul at the beginning of a passage which expounds membership of the body of Christ with differing gifts: "I appeal to you, brethren, by the mercies of God, to present your bodies as a living sacrifice, holy and acceptable to God, which is your spiritual worship" (Romans 12.1). To be renewed in worship must also mean to be renewed in mission.

To ask if a charismatic congregation is more successful in its mission than a non-charismatic one is too crude a question. Mission is a notoriously difficult activity to evaluate. Taking a large geographical area over a period of time we might argue that the policies of the European-based missions to Africa in the nineteenth century robbed them of greater effectiveness, and that the missions of the Pentecostal Churches in South America since the beginning of the twentieth century have been spectacularly fruitful, but an assessment of one particular congregation's mission over a few years is almost an impossibility.

In 1977 the Archbishops' Council on Evangelism published a profile of an anonymous parish in the north of England which had been studied as a research project by an American visitor. A series of graphs showed how the congregation had developed in recent years and how the various sexes and age-groups were represented in it. The period of growth began after what the report described as "a change of incumbent followed by a subdued charismatic awakening and consolidated in a shift of pastoral and outreach strategy from centralised congregation to multiplied house groups." The most rapid increase in the congregation happened among young couples in the 20–34 years age-group. The average number of weekly communicants was 30 or so between 1955 and 1965, then it began to increase until it was 110 in 1975. But most remarkable of all was the annual giving in cash. From 1955 to 1970 it hovered around the £1,000 mark. Then it leapt up in a series of dramatic bounds: £5,000 in 1971, £6,500 in 1972, £9,000 in 1973, £16,000 in 1974, and well over £20,000 in 1975.

Even with these statistics before us it is still not easy to employ the word "successful". But what is interesting is that the mission of the parish church became more effective when a new incumbent arrived who was himself renewed in the Holy Spirit. The pattern has been repeated elsewhere. It has been demonstrated that the pastor is nearly always the one who decides the attitude of a congregation to its mission. If he is himself alive to God's call and opportunities, the mission of the local church will begin to unfold. But if he is hesitant, lazy, or unbelieving, its mission will falter.

Many of today's pastors, especially those in responsible posts, have received their formation in a theological world that ruthlessly questioned the nature of the Church's mission. The academic argument went something like this: "The Christian mission must be set in the wider picture of man's struggle for survival and social justice.—The world therefore sets the Church's agenda for its mission.—Christians witness most effectively to their Lord by a concern for the needy and underprivileged.—To try and bring a man or a woman to a personal commitment to Christ without first caring about the circumstances within which that individual lives is to make a mockery of the Gospel.—Jesus Christ is 'the man for others', the revolutionary, the suffering servant of God who through his passion and death identified himself with human misery.—The Church must go into the world and do likewise."

Although Christians with evangelical sympathies rejected this theology of mission, it has been influential in much that was taught in colleges and seminaries in the last twenty-five years, and it has guided the policies of departments of missions in the denominational structures. It was also behind much of the thinking on mission produced by the World Council of Churches in the 'sixties. In more recent years, however, its influence has begun to wane. Some of its students discovered its inadequacy in their own experience of mission in different parts of the world, especially when contrasted with the more evangelical and Pentecostal forms of evangelism.

Howard Corry, general secretary of the New Zealand Student Christian Movement, was for some years involved in the Waikiki mission, an ecumenical attempt by the churches of Hawaii to be of service to people in the area. The social problems were appalling, from the destitutes who had been lured to Honolulu by romantic stories of an easy life in the sun to the drug addicts, alcoholics and criminals in a neighbourhood known as "The Jungle". The strategy of the mission changed from time to time. At one point Howard Corry was wandering through the streets at night wearing a clerical collar, counselling any who approached him; later an emphasis was placed on community development, helping people to organise themselves to secure the services they needed—a free drug clinic, a drop-in refuge in an abandoned church building, a youth hostel and a multi-purpose community centre. The Waikiki mission was closed in 1974 because of financial constraints.

Looking back on his experiences, Howard Corry reflected that one of the faults of the Waikiki mission had been that it had depended too much on the Protestant "secular theology" with the kind of interpretation of mission that I have just outlined. "We were out to bring the kingdom of God all by ourselves," he wrote. "Our witness to God's love was genuine but unbalanced and incomplete. We served but hardly ever prayed, listened to people's

problems but seldom spoke of Christ, organised food coopera-
tives but not eucharists."* He went on to confess that he came to
admire those Christians who live in the confidence that God has
enough grace for all our needs.

If the missionary thrust of a local church has been impeded by
the pastor's theology of mission, it has also been blunted by a
gnawing sense of doubt that many Christians have about their
faith. They wonder if Christianity really works. They accept that
perhaps it did in a less sophisticated age, but they feel that the
advance of modern scientific knowledge has shaken the foundations of their belief. They question whether God really cares in
the way the scriptures say he does. They query the reality of Jesus
Christ and the Gospel. They are uneasy about some of the things
taught by the Church. Indeed, there is a widespread assumption
that faith itself can be explained more in terms of upbringing and
psychological make-up than of free choice and inward turning.
Consequently, these doubting Christians are God-shy. They are
shy of the word itself; they are shy of the Being represented by that
word. It is interesting to notice how many tend to avoid using
"God" and "Jesus Christ" in their conversations, even when
talking about religious matters. To use a phrase like, "The Lord
led me to do this," embarrasses them. Although they want to
believe in the risen Christ, they find it hard to look you straight
in the eyes when you talk about Jesus as a living, present reality.

This God-shyness is found among some pastors as well.
Although they may have grown up or been converted to a real
faith in Jesus Christ, this has often been challenged during the
course of their studies in preparation for ordination. It is no doubt
necessary that the future teachers of Christian doctrine should be
aware of the speculations of contemporary scholars, but it is an
unfortunate fact of experience that many students acquire a certain amount of theological information while they are at college at
the cost of losing some faith. If a college is not itself a Spirit-filled
community—a difficult achievement when we consider the
nature of such colleges, with their rapid turnover of members and
with the tensions that inevitably arise from such a demanding
lifestyle—then individuals leave without the spiritual foundations on which they can build their ministry. This is why

* *One World* (World Council of Churches, Geneva) No. 31,
November 1977, p. 20.

preachers of the Pentecostal Churches used to refer to college seminaries as "cemeteries".

The ordinand who emerges from this training as a spiritual casualty rather than a spiritual leader often does not have a chance to rediscover the reality of God's power in his own life before he is given a pastoral responsibility. He may be a good man. He may be concerned for people. He may demonstrate the love of God through his care for the sick and needy and through his involvement in community activities. He may be respected in the neighbourhood as one of those who can be trusted as a friend in need. He may win the affection and gratitude of his congregation. But he is not able to encourage faith in others. He cannot speak as if the risen Christ was the most important person in his life. His sermons are expositions of the scriptures culled from the lectures he attended at college or discussions about the latest theological debates. He can say little about Christianity as a way of living in the power of the Holy Spirit. The result is that his goodness is attributed to his personality rather than to his Lord.

I hope that many who read the last few paragraphs will be prompted to say, "Yes, it was like that, but it's changing now." There are encouraging signs. The denominations are recovering a confidence in proclaiming the Gospel of the Kingdom. They are less inclined to be swayed in their faith by the speculations of theologians. It is noteworthy that the publication of *The Myth of God Incarnate* in 1977 had nothing like the effect on ordinary church folk as the radical books of the 'sixties did. Pastors and congregations are realising afresh that faith does not depend on the wisdom of even the most brilliant men but on the gift of God. Not a little of this recovery is due to the direct and indirect influence of the charismatic movement. Distinguished leaders like Cardinal Leon Suenens and Bishop Michael Ramsay have used their teaching skills to demonstrate how personal renewal in the Holy Spirit can strengthen the Christian in the established denominations and equip him for his witness in the world. It is no longer possible to accuse the charismatic movement of being anti-intellectual in the presentation of the faith. Rather, it has highlighted a truth which has been acknowledged by leading Christian teachers in every age, that a theology which is not itself a manifestation of the Holy Spirit is dead.

The denominations have been given fresh encouragement by

recent pronouncements on mission from their leaders and representatives. The years 1974–75 saw three important international Christian gatherings concerned with this subject. In 1974 two thousand Evangelicals meeting in Lausanne and representing 150 nations issued a Covenant calling on all Christians to work together for the evangelisation of the world. In the same year the bishops of the Roman Catholic Church met in synod under the Pope to discuss the same topic, and later the Pope published an Apostolic Exhortation urging Christians "to risk their lives so that the Kingdom may be proclaimed and the Church established in the midst of the world." Then in 1975 the fifth assembly of the World Council of Churches in Nairobi examined the implications of mission in the section of its report entitled "Confessing Christ Today".

What is interesting for our purposes is that all three documents from these widely differing Christian traditions focus on the Holy Spirit as the source and power of mission.

> The Holy Spirit is a missionary Spirit; thus evangelism should arise spontaneously from a Spirit-filled Church. A Church that is not a missionary Church is contradicting itself and quenching the Spirit. Worldwide evangelism will become a realistic possibility only when the Spirit renews the Church in truth and wisdom, faith, holiness, love and power. We call upon all Christians to pray for such a visitation of the sovereign Spirit of God that all his fruit may appear in all his people and that all his gifts may enrich the body of Christ.

> It must be said that the Holy Spirit is the principal agent in evangelism: it is he who impels each individual to proclaim the Gospel, and it is he who in the depths of consciences causes the word of salvation to be accepted and understood. But it can equally be said that he is the goal of salvation: he alone stirs up the new creation, the new humanity of which evangelisation is to be the result, with that unity in variety which evangelisation wishes to achieve within the Christian community.

> Jesus Christ is the faithful witness to God (Revelation 1.5). In his self-offering on the cross he redeems us from sin and godless powers and reconciles creation with God. Therefore

we shall live for God and shall be saved in God. "There is no condemnation for those who are in Christ Jesus, who walk not after the flesh, but after the Spirit" (Romans 8.1). We believe with certainty in the presence and guidance of the Holy Spirit, who proceeds from the Father and bears witness to Christ (John 15.26). Our witness to Christ is made strong in the Holy Spirit and alive in the confessing community of the Church.

It would be difficult to find a more Pentecostal approach to mission than in these passages. It is even difficult to distinguish who said which (for the record, the first is from Lausanne, the second from Pope Paul, and the third from Nairobi).* The Pope added, "Each one of us is called in our baptism to confess Christ according to the special charism which one has received from God." Charismatics feel that here is the heart of what they understand mission to be—what each member is led and equipped by the Holy Spirit to undertake.

Out of the discussions on a theology of mission, then, there has emerged a charismatic view of the nature of the Church. What we are learning—and for this we owe much to the theologians of "the Third Church"—is that the Church does not "have" a mission. Rather, the mission of Jesus Christ creates the Church. Worship and mission are part of one another because both are expressions of the Church herself as her members respond to her Lord. Mission, therefore, does not come from the Church; it is from mission and in the light of mission that the Church has to be understood. The whole congregation and every member within it belong with all their spiritual gifts and potential charisms to the mission of God's kingdom. The concept of an every-member ministry means that the whole congregation is missionary, not just a few individuals in it. Mission will happen as we mature in the Holy Spirit, as we realise more and more that it is the Spirit in us who bears witness to the risen Lord. Everything about us in our local church—our worship, our relationships, our attitudes to others, especially the strangers among us—will speak of Jesus Christ. The total life of a congregation will be both an evangelistic proc-

* *The Lausanne Covenant*, 14 (*International Review of Missions*, Vol. 63, No. 252, World Council of Churches, Geneva, October 1974, p. 573); *Evangelisation in the Modern World*: Apostolic Exhortation of His Holiness Pope Paul VI, 75 (Catholic Truth Society, 1976, p. 106); *Breaking Barriers: Nairobi 1975*, David M. Paton (ed.) (SPCK, 1976) p. 44.

lamation of God in the neighbourhood and also a community of love in a world that experiences very little of unmerited love from other people.

It happens in spite of our weaknesses. As I have indicated, congregations that are trying to walk more obediently in the Spirit are not necessarily fellowships where joy and harmony are always found. Like individuals, they have their ups and downs—and the ups and downs tend to become more extreme when they are in the process of spiritual renewal. Indeed, I know of no local church that did not go through considerable difficulties and testing after it had advanced in the surge of the charismatic movement. What witnesses to the power of God in a congregation is not the sense of joy and harmony but the love which enables its members to contain and conquer personal tensions and weaknesses among them. Society is familiar with the spectacle of a group of people quarrelling and dividing because of differences between them; it is not familiar with the spectacle of a group of people experiencing differences among themselves and then going on to love one another into a stronger unity. That is what is ultimately evangelistic in a local church.

Does this mean that there is no place for organised evangelistic campaigns, either on a large scale like Billy Graham's, or in a local neighbourhood with a visiting preacher?

Before we try to answer this question, we must briefly consider the ministry of an evangelist in the Church. The evangelist is listed third after apostles and prophets in Ephesians 4.11, and Timothy was urged to do the work of an evangelist in fulfilment of his ministry (2 Timothy 4.5). But the most vivid picture of an evangelist's role is given in the description of Philip's activity in Acts 8.5–7 where he proclaimed the Gospel of the kingdom and signs followed in the casting out of unclean spirits and the healing of the sick. The early church historian Eusebius saw the ministry continuing in those who "built on the foundations of the churches everywhere laid by the apostles, spreading the message still further and sowing the saving seed of the kingdom of heaven far and wide throughout the entire world . . . Leaving their homes behind, they carried out the work of evangelists, ambitious to preach to those who had never yet heard the message of faith."*

* Eusebius, *The History of the Church*, iii, 37 (*Penguin Classics*, 1965, p. 148).

The ministry of an evangelist has never been established as an office in the Church like the ministries of bishops, presbyters and deacons. It remains a charismatic gift to individuals rather than a formal ministry in the institutional sense, and as such it is discerned thankfully by Christians who appreciate the spiritual gifts in those like Billy Graham who have been used by God to proclaim the Gospel. They also discern the gift in those who teach Jesus Christ through other media—plays, pictures and other dramatic productions. But the charismatic renewal has helped us to look at ordinary Christians in local churches with the hope that among them this spiritual gift would be exercised—corporately as well as by individuals.

A weakness of the old-style evangelistic campaign is that it tends to leave congregations with the impression that the proclamation of the Gospel is the business of the visiting evangelist rather than theirs. No matter how carefully the follow-up is planned after the campaign is over—and no notable evangelist neglects this vital aspect of the work—the missionary thrust of a local church still peters out when the visitors have left. Perhaps it is fortunate that the Church has never created a permanent office round the charism of an evangelist. Experience suggests that when one person is given a special responsibility for some aspect of the Church's ministry, the rest of the congregation readily opt out of it!

It is in order to encourage evangelistic gifts within the local churches that visits by outside teams these days are aimed at encouraging the congregations rather than converting the enquirers who attend the meetings and rallies. Titles like "crusade" and "campaign" are avoided in order to show that these projects are something different. David Watson has led with a team from his church in York festivals or celebrations with greater accent on rejoicing in the risen Lord rather than urging the unconverted to accept Jesus Christ as their Saviour. In an age when people are reached more through what they see rather than what they hear, the joyful celebration of the Christian faith through dance and the proclamation of the Gospel through drama, in streets, schools and public halls rather than in church buildings, has proved to be more effective than the form of evangelistic outreach which became popular in the nineteenth century revivals and which has continued down to our own day. The York team has conducted festivals in Leeds, Newcastle, Belfast and Manchester using these means of celebration and proclamation with huge congregations. These festivals owe much to the style and format of the big charismatic prayer meetings such as those organised by the Fountain Trust under the title *Glory in the Church*. A similar ministry is fulfilled by the Fisherfolk of the Community of Celebration based at Post Green.

It is helpful to see these festivals as occasional local additions to the Church's calendar. During Holy Week and Easter each year Christians commemorate and celebrate the passion, death and resurrection of Jesus Christ and all that these saving acts mean for us today. With the aid of scripture readings, hymns, canticles, drama, music, visual presentations and sermons, congregations are encouraged to respond more faithfully in their lives to what God has done and is doing for them through Jesus Christ by the power of the Holy Spirit. The fact that these saving events are commemorated and celebrated only for one week during the year does not mean that they are forgotten at other times. On the contrary, concentrating on them for one day or one week helps us to appropriate to ourselves the grace of these saving events at all times, so that every day becomes a day of dying and rising with Christ. Now the festivals such as I have mentioned fulfil a similar role. By celebrating our membership of the Church as a new life in the Holy Spirit during one week—assisted, perhaps, by a visit from a team—we are encouraged to engage in every ministry, including evangelism, that is offered us through the charisms in the congregation at other times.

Setting the ministry of the evangelist within the team or community of the local church is altogether desirable. It discourages the cult of the personality. It emphasises that such ministries are within the body of Christ. We shall note this same pattern when we discuss the ministry of healing in the next chapter—and, indeed, it can be applied to all ministries (including that of the pastor whose ministry, as we have seen, is enriched when it is shared with those who exercise a charismatic leadership within the congregation). Spiritual gifts are more clearly manifested to be *for* the body of Christ when they are seen to be *within* the Church.

At St. Andrew's, Chorleywood, Hertfordshire, one of the priests on the staff has a special responsibility for evangelism—not to be *the* evangelist but to assist the members of the congregation to be evangelistic. Groups representing a wide cross-section of its membership visit other local churches for weekends and weeks in faith-sharing projects. The team can number up to forty, and it is engaged in this ministry about once a month, invitations being received from all over England. A "Focus on Faith" fortnight in Hazelmere, Buckinghamshire, was based on sixty house groups and involved one hundred members of St. Andrew's Church, together with drama and music groups. This strategy of using the members of one congregation to encourage the members of another to be evangelistic seems particularly appropriate in a movement that is enabling the laity to fulfil their mission in the power of the Holy Spirit. And it is a pointer for the denominations. Their general policy has been to open up new work by sending into an area a lone and often unsupported clergyman, who was expected to build up a congregation from the people he found living or working there. No wonder this policy has so often failed, leaving ordained men exhausted, disillusioned, and perhaps suffering from a nervous breakdown! The mission of the Church was never intended to be the responsibility of an individual working on his own.

I was once a member of an ecumenical planning committee that had been set up to examine how the denominations were to act if a large urban development was built to create a new town in what was then open countryside. After seeking the advice of those who had lived and worked in other new towns, we decided that we would not initially attempt to build two or three new churches and appoint pastors to them (although this was an attractive suggestion to those of us who were keen that the denominations should go into the urban development as a united group and establish ecumenical congregations there from the beginning). Instead, we agreed to recommend that what money was available should be used to purchase ordinary houses in groups at two or three strategic places, and that committed Christian families from other parts of the county should be invited to move into them. We hoped that the members of these families would be so brought together by the Lord that they would between them have the necessary spiritual gifts for this missionary task and would be the beginnings of new congregations. We left open for a while the question of whether or not any of the husbands of these families should be ordained. Unfortunately, this large urban development never materialised.

There is not an opportunity here to describe how the charismatic renewal is revitalising the local church's mission in a neighbourhood in service and social involvement. But it is one of the signs that follows a spiritual renewal in a congregation that it is used to bring the healing power of Jesus Christ to a sick world. Some of the earliest charismatic groups I met in the early sixties soon found themselves caring for people with drug addiction, alcoholism, emotional breakdowns, and the other spiritual and mental diseases of our society. One group developed into a community to provide a home for troubled individuals needing long-term support. The pattern is being followed elsewhere. From their experiences in this kind of mission, charismatics have had to face the devil in his various dark manifestations. This has not only been evident through the ministry of deliverance to individuals, but also in situations like Northern Ireland, where charismatic prayer groups consisting of Catholics and Protestants have been made aware that they are struggling "against the principalities, against the powers". A generation ago many Christians would have dismissed as primitive fantasies suggestions that evil spiritual forces influenced the destinies of men and societies. But not today.

No congregation in the Western world can fail to recognise that the Church has an important mission in helping people to live responsibly in our multi-racial society. Although a local church may not have families of other ethnic origins actually living in its neighbourhood, there can be no congregation that does not have some members involved with such families either through schooling, employment, or more informal contacts. The Christian approaches those of other races with the knowledge that God's promise to pour out his Spirit on *all* flesh was fulfilled on the day of Pentecost, and that every individual of another culture and another religion is one who, created in God's image, is within the range of Christ's saving grace, and who may be a person through whom God can reveal himself by his Spirit. The charismatic should be particularly sensitive to this truth. And then there is another point of contact for him. Many of the black-led local churches that are to be found in English and American cities are Pentecostal in tradition (to be distinguished by the bewildering variety of their names), and the charismatic should find in their exuberant worship and warm fellowship much that is familiar to him—especially the Pentecostal gifts of prayer.

Walter Hollenweger warns us that in Pentecostal circles race is a crucial issue. Black Pentecostals in America are suspicious, not only of white Christians of other denominations, but also of white Pentecostals for their half-hearted opposition to racism. He quotes a pastor of the Assemblies of God in Alabama who said, "I feel that the greatest indictment against the Church of the Lord Jesus in our country is our stand (or lack of it) on racial problems." In England there are still too many Christians who fail to see that such a stand requires political action as well as fervent prayer. The local anti-race committee could be the place for as powerful a manifestation of the Holy Spirit as the charismatic prayer meeting. It is remarkable how a word of loving reconciliation from Christians on such committees can have shattering effects, especially after the ranting of the extremists. In elections—for local government as well as for Parliament—candidates must be made to declare where they themselves stand on this issue. The lesson from America is shouted across the Atlantic. The historian of the Pentecostal Assemblies of the World, Morris E. Golder, contrasts the Baptist Martin Luther King and his liberating ministry with the high-flung statements of the Pentecostals on the power of the Holy Spirit. "If the white Pentecostal brethren would have stood firm against prejudice and racial injustice, having the most powerful authority (the Holy Spirit) and the most powerful message (the gospel of Jesus Christ), they could have been the instruments of God for the destruction of this hideous ideology. But instead of fighting against it, they submitted to its influence and have been affected by it even until now."* English Christians still have a chance—and, led by the Spirit, some of them are taking it. More can share in this struggle for human dignity. If charismatics affirm that authentic liberation can never occur apart from a genuine encounter with the Holy Spirit, they ought also to affirm that no man can experience the fullness of the Spirit and at the same time be a racist.

The mission of a congregation renewed by the Holy Spirit will not always be as spectacular as this in a neighbourhood. Often it

* Quotations from Walter Hollenweger, *Pentecost between Black and White* (Christian Journals Limited, Belfast, 1974) pp. 21–2.

will be more hidden. There is a danger of being swept onto a particular bandwaggon just because everybody is saying that it is the greatest need in society today. We must remember that the Church's mission does not spring from a desire that the Church should be seen to be relevant. Too often when the Church tries to be relevant it becomes secularised and drifts into humanism. Howard Corry's reflections remind us that when Christians have great ideas for social service in their neighbourhood and ask God to bless those ideas, they fail because they weren't the Lord's ideas at all. Relevance in mission begins with God.

"A charismatic approach to social issues does not limit itself to a narrow list of issues, dictated by the secular establishment. Amidst all the clamour of the social arena, it seeks to be sensitive to those concerns which the Lord himself sets before his Church."*

* Larry Christenson, *A Charismatic Approach to Social Action* (Lakeland, 1975) p. 34.

11
Healing

The Church has never completely lost the vision that hers is a ministry of healing, but her members' concept of that ministry has varied with the progress of medical science. Up until fairly recent times, when it seemed that there was no physical or psychological disorder that could not be cured one day through treatment, the Church generally surrendered much of the responsibility for this ministry to the medical profession. The sick were prayed for by name, visited, given Communion and encouraged; not many pastors or members of their congregations envisaged a more direct ministry that included invocations for healing with anointing and the laying on of hands.

Here and there little groups of Christians launched out into a more direct healing ministry. The Guild of St. Raphael and the Guild of Health were sponsored by the members of different denominations to encourage prayer with anointing and the laying on of hands, and communities like the Dorothy Kerin Home of Healing at Burrswood and the Divine Healing Mission at Crowhurst were established to promote the ministry of healing. Gradually the Church began to recognise officially that this ministry meant more than a few prayers for the sick during worship. Forms of services for this purpose have been approved in most provinces of the Anglican Communion during the last thirty or forty years, and following Vatican II the Roman Catholic Church has provided a liturgy for the sick which includes the laying on of hands, anointing, and prayers for healing. Yet without the impetus given to it by the charismatic movement, it is doubtful whether this ministry would have developed so widely among the denominations as it has done today. For if the charismatic movement is known best of all for the practice of speaking in tongues, its next most well-known feature is prayer for healing. Even congregations that look on the movement with suspicion accept this ministry thankfully and with joy.

The subject is a large one and many books have been written on it in the last few years. I have no intention of expounding the theological reasons for the exercise of this ministry in the contemporary Church nor of discussing the many problems associated with it. Here I will raise only a few points connected with the way it is discerned and exercised within the life of a congregation.

The weakness of the less direct form of the ministry of healing—the occasional prayers in church and the encouraging visits to the patient—is that it tends to push the sick to the fringe of the congregation's concern. The result is a sort of spiritual hospitalisation. The congregation remembers the individual by name on Sundays, arranges a visit to his home or the hospital (or leaves it to the pastor to do this), and then busies itself with other things. But scripturally the ministry of healing is in the vanguard of the Church's mission. In the Bible salvation is more than the forgiveness of personal sin; it is being made whole in everything that goes to make us what we are. The healing acts of Jesus liberated man from all that could bind him, beginning with the spiritual, psychological and physical disorders from which he suffered, but then going on to those circumstances within which he lived. The Gospel of the kingdom is aimed at man in all his dimensions. God's kingdom, it has been said, is creation restored. That is why Christ came not only with authority to preach but also to forgive, to drive out demons and to heal. And it was on this same mission that he sent his disciples by the power of the Holy Spirit.

The ministry of healing, then, needs to be seen not on the fringe of a congregation's concern but in the very centre of its missionary activity. And in a congregation which is being renewed by the Spirit, this is where it begins to establish itself. For with a growing sensitivity towards the needs of ordinary people—a sensitivity that stems from a greater openness to the love of God—it becomes more and more evident that the things that ravage lives today are those which must be exposed and dealt with through the ministry of healing in all its aspects. In modern society many experience rejection, alienation, psychological abuse, emotional warfare and emptiness—probably on a scale never experienced before in the history of mankind. Our plastic age with its frenzied activity, constant mobility and technological nightmares, is leaving behind it a ruin of hollow men and women. Never before has it been more necessary to proclaim the glorious message of the Kingdom: the Father cares, Christ has come and is coming, the Spirit reconciles and heals. Never before has it been more necessary for the Church to demonstrate in practical ways its faith in the power of the Holy Trinity.

Individual Christians do have special charisms for the exercise of this ministry. The lessons of the charismatic movement have made us more conscious of this and more alert to the possibility that such individuals are being gifted by God in our own congregations. But the charismatic movement is also teaching us that gifts of healing can be expected in answer to prayers by anyone, and this means that we should exercise the ministry within the fellowship of the local church. Indeed, an important part of that healing ministry will be the individual's experience of the congregation as a community which is both experiencing and ministering healing.

In this way those with a special charism are saved from being regarded as "a spiritual healer"—with all the misunderstandings and dangers such a title invokes. Like the evangelist, their ministry is seen to be set within the body of Christ, and those who seek that ministry are encouraged to look to the Lord present in his Church rather than to the gift exercised by the individual. Also, different needs create different ministries. One who has a charism for ministering to certain kinds of illnesses may not be the one who can minister to other disorders. It is not uncommon to find those with a special gift for the ministry of healing themselves specialising in the kinds of people they are called on to help. This should not surprise us. Specialisation is a general feature of life, and if the Lord works this way in the natural gifts he bestows, we should expect him to do the same in the distribution of spiritual gifts. When the whole congregation is involved in the ministry of healing, these specialisations begin to emerge.

In the Barnabas Fellowship at Whatcombe House we noticed how certain people with particular needs among those who visited us seemed to be drawn to individual members of the community. Those who need counselling in depth with prayer gravitated towards the warden, Reg East, whereas those requiring prayer with the laying on of hands for more straightforward illnesses went to other members of the community. Unhappy folk troubled with forms of evil disturbance usually went to one or two who were experienced in the ministry of deliverance. Thus the ministry became a community activity rather than one exercised by a few individuals. We worked in pairs or teams and, in this way, learned much from one another. But within the pair or team, the member who had the special charism for ministering to the particular need that manifested itself took the initiative.

A congregation or community can provide that continuous support and encouragement that is necessary in many cases. The healing of individuals in body, mind and spirit is rarely an instantaneous business. They need to be reassured again and again of the love of Jesus Christ through his Church. Only slowly do those who feel pain, frustration, oppression, shame, cowardice, resentment and despair find them replaced by the fruit of the Spirit.

Let us examine this corporate ministry in three areas of the ministry of healing that have become better known through the charismatic movement—prayer counselling, deliverance, and services of prayer for healing.

Prayer counselling (sometimes called healing of the memories or inner healing) is when a Christian—or, better, two Christians—assist another to talk through his problems with the expectation that God will disclose the root of the trouble and heal the effect it has had on his life. Those who listen believe that if they are open to the Holy Spirit he will, through his charisms, enable them to discern what is wrong and to invoke the healing grace of Jesus Christ. This usually means sessions in which the individual describes his past, his earliest memories and impressions, his relationships as a child with his parents and those nearest to him, as well as his more recent experiences. The counsellors give him their fullest attention. "We let them talk while we enter as understandingly and imaginatively as we are able into what they are saying and expressing. Our concentration is to try to understand what it is like to be *them*."* It is a delicate and costly ministry. It requires much patience and accurate discernment. That is why two listeners can be more effective than one. They can check each other's reactions and be more objective without being less caring.

Slowly the spiritual gifts begin to manifest themselves in the listeners. A gift of knowledge illuminates a dark area of a troubled

* Reginald East, *Heal the Sick* (Hodder and Stoughton, 1977) p. 88.

life. An inspired picture points to a factor that the individual has overlooked. A question asked on impulse jogs the memory and shakes up a crucial circumstance. The whole past that created the situation within which the individual suffered hurts and rejections is recalled and faced. Then the prayers are offered by the counsellors—for the forgiveness of offences long overlooked, for the healing of hurts that caused pain to go down into the deep consciousness. The healing of Jesus Christ is invoked into the bad relationships, the terrifying memories, the black dreams, the evil experiences that scarred mind and spirit. The individual is assured that Jesus, who is the beginning and the end, the Lord of all time, can heal what is past and seal him with his grace for the future.

What is offered is the ministry of a spiritual comforter—a comforter, that is, in the scriptural sense of *paracletos*, one who stands by to help and support in the name of Jesus Christ. A significant number of those who have been baptised in the Spirit and who are maturing in their relationships with others find themselves ministering in this way. There is nothing formal about it. Relatives, friends, acquaintances, sometimes strangers, sense that here is a man or a woman who in a mysterious way is like a strong tower beside them. They feel impelled to confide in them. "Can I have a chat with you about something that's bothering me?" is usually the only indication that this ministry is being asked for. Often the request comes at a very inconvenient moment! But what the needy one is seeking—although he may not identify it as such at the time—is Jesus Christ the bringer of forgiveness and healing who is revealing himself through the Christian by the Holy Spirit.

As more members of a congregation are trained for this ministry (spiritual gifts should be encouraged and supported by the insights offered through counsellor-training) the pastor is relieved of what can be a heavy burden. In recent years there has been an increasing use of the clergy as counsellors. The denominations have provided post-ordination courses with this in view (in England through bodies like the Clinical Theology Association and the Westminster Pastoral Foundation) and this ministry takes up much of a pastor's time. While many individuals have been helped, there is a danger that the pastors concerned are diverted from other tasks which—from the viewpoint of their ministry in the congregation—may well be more important. If pastors spend long hours each week listening to individuals with problems they will have little energy left for their presiding ministry within a congregation's life—the preparation of worship and teaching, the time they spend with individuals and groups, personal prayer and study.

Gifted and trained members of the congregation can fulfil this ministry very successfully given the right kind of encouragement and oversight. They do not have to be educated in a narrowly academic way: folk with some experience of life and an openness to the Spirit of God can act as a prayer counsellor for others from different backgrounds. It is sometimes assumed that in order to help a person with scientific qualifications you must find a Christian with some knowledge in this field to help him. This is certainly not true. What matters is the spirituality and the sensitivity of the counsellor, not his intellectual capabilities or specialist knowledge. When a team of counsellors begins to form in a congregation, the pastor keeps in touch with who is counselling whom—this guards against the practice that some troubled people adopt of shopping around with their problems—and only steps in to the actual counselling sessions when his particular authority or guidance is required.

The ministry of deliverance is now being recognised as a branch of the healing work of the Church that cannot be dismissed as it was a few years ago. There are certain people whose problems can only be dealt with in this way. More than almost any other healing ministry it needs a team to undertake it. The Christian who attempts to minister deliverance by himself runs grave risks of self-deception and spiritual danger. It requires a period of discernment to test carefully the source of the problem. It entails the preparation of those who minister and of the person concerned with repentance, prayer and sometimes fasting. After the individual has confessed his sins, renounced evil and forgiven all injuries, he affirms his faith in Jesus Christ as his Lord and Saviour, and then those with him bind the spirit and command it to depart in the name of Christ. The process may be long or short, but it frequently culminates in some sign that the person has been delivered. There is always a distinct sense of peace and often a change in the facial appearance: a new light comes into the eyes and the lines of tension soften. When these signs appear, the group pray for the healing and infilling of the Holy Spirit, that the victory of Christ might be established in the life of the one who has been delivered.

It is unfortunate that this ministry has been sensationalised in the news media as a result of one or two unfortunate cases. A few years ago a man in Bradford committed suicide after a group had attempted to deliver him from some evil influence, and this prompted the bishops of the Church of England to issue instructions that no further exorcisms were to be attempted without permission. Happily not all of them were content with this negative reaction. In some dioceses they called together groups of clergy and laity to give advice on this ministry, and there are now opportunities both in the Anglican Church and in other denominations for those who find themselves involved in cases needing deliverance to seek support. Groups in congregations with little knowledge or experience should *always* seek outside help before they attempt a ministry of deliverance with a troubled person. The key to this ministry is the charism of discernment of spirits, and this is one of the most difficult of the spiritual gifts to test. That is why outside assistance is necessary.

After prayer counselling and deliverance physical healing often follows. Some people, of course, require only prayer for physical healing, though it may be necessary to counsel the individual first. In cases where confidentiality has to be maintained, this kind of prayer can only be offered privately—though it is usually better to have at least two ministering rather than one, even if the individual concerned makes a private confession to the pastor alone as the first step. Otherwise there is everything to be said for prayer with the laying on of hands and perhaps also anointing to be ministered within the setting of the congregation's worship. I have already noted one or two ways in which this can be done.

Services of prayer for healing have become more common in recent years. They demonstrate that the congregation is a community concerned with healing, and they meet a need that is widespread at the present time when more people are realising that medical care itself is fulfilled within the Church's healing ministry. I have used the following form of service on many occasions and found it very satisfactory with both large and small congregations:

Service of Prayer for Healing

Introduction
  Hymn
  Notices
  Preparatory prayer
Ministry of the Word of God
  Scripture reading
  Hymn, psalm, canticle or song
  Scripture reading
  Address
Ministry of Prayer for Healing
  General confession and absolution
  Affirmation of faith
  Intercessions
  Hymn
  Laying on of hands (and anointing)
  Hymn
  Dismissal

What to call the service is a minor problem. Titles like, "A Service of Healing" or "A Healing Service" seem to me to be open to misunderstanding. They either suggest that everyone is going to be healed at the service (though we may hope for this, there are ways of receiving the Lord's healing grace which demand greater faith than that of looking for an instant, automatic near-miracle), or they have associations with "spiritual healers" that are unhelpful, if not damaging. "A Service of Prayer for Healing" or "A Celebration of the Ministry of Healing" are longer titles but more accurate descriptions of what a congregation is concerned with in these gatherings.

The service is designed on the pattern of the four elements that we have already described—introduction, ministry of the Word of God, response, and dismissal.

The *Introduction* consists of items that enable people to learn why they have come together and to begin to look expectantly at God.

(1) *Hymn.* This should be wellknown, affirming faith in God for his redemption of the world by Jesus Christ and expressing hope in his grace.

(2) *Notices.* The pastor, or the one who is leading the service,

explains what is going to happen, making sure that all who are participating know what they are to do and why. This is especially important for two groups of people in the congregation, (*a*) those who are going to pray aloud for the sick by name (see item 10) and (*b*) those who are going to receive the laying on of hands (see item 12). It is also necessary to make certain practical details clear, e.g. where the congregation is to stand, sit and kneel, and what they are to respond during the intercessions (*Lord, hear our prayer—And let our cry come unto you*, or some other suitable formulary).

(3) *Preparatory prayer*. The pastor and the congregation ask God to send the Holy Spirit to guide and equip them for this ministry.

The *Ministry of the Word of God* has the same purpose here as in any liturgy—to enable the congregation to listen to the Lord at the commencement of their worship.

(4) *Scripture reading*. If suitable passages do not come to mind, the official lectionaries of the Churches should be consulted. Silence may be kept for a few moments afterwards.

(5) *Hymn, psalm, canticle or song*. A solo or choir anthem is often appropriate here. The congregation remains sitting in a quiet, reflective mood, waiting for the next reading.

(6) *Scripture reading*. Sometimes a suitable passage from a non-biblical book may be read.

(7) *The Address*. The scriptures are expounded to encourage the congregation to respond in faith to God's love and power. Christ's promise that the Father hears the prayers of his children are an important part of this exposition. It is essential to stress that everyone must offer himself from his heart to accept in thankfulness whatever God wills for him. Bitterness and depression are stumbling-blocks on the road to healing, for they indicate that we are looking at ourselves and not at the Lord. It may be appropriate to invite someone who has been healed to give a brief testimony at this point.

The *Ministry of Prayer for Healing* builds up into the response of the congregation to the Word of God. It corresponds to the ministry of the sacrament in the liturgy of the eucharist.

(8) *General confession and absolution*. Acts of penitence and declarations of God's forgiveness that are familiar to the congregation should be used. There is much to be said for borrowing

these forms from other services commonly celebrated in the local church—it strengthens the impression that the service of prayer for healing is another facet of the congregation's worship.

(9) *Affirmation of faith.* This can be made by using sentences from scripture, the creed, or by inviting the congregation to re-affirm the questions put to them at baptism, e.g. "Do you believe in God the Father who made you and all the world? . . . Do you believe in his Son Jesus Christ who redeemed you and all mankind? . . . Do you believe in the Holy Spirit who sanctifies you and all the people of God? . . ."

(10) *Intercessions.* Individual members of the congregation are invited to pray aloud briefly for any sick they know. The pastor explains here or in the *Notices* that they can say a few words of explanation to begin with if it will help others to envisage the needs of the one they are praying for. The prayer should be offered directly to God with an indication when the congregation are to make a response. The result might sound like this: "*(To the congregation)* I'd like to pray for Peter. He's my younger brother, and he is in hospital waiting for an operation . . . *(To God)* Father, I ask you to touch Peter with your healing grace, that he may praise you and serve you through your Son Jesus Christ. Lord, in your mercy . . . Hear our prayer." In some church buildings open intercessions are difficult because of acoustic problems, but participation by the congregation like this builds up the sense that the ministry of healing is an act of the whole Body of Christ, not just the work of the pastor.

(11) *Hymn.* The congregation should be invited to kneel or sit during the intercessions and the laying on of hands (item 12). If these activities are prolonged, the opportunity to stand for a hymn at this point will be welcomed.

(12) *Laying on of hands (and anointing).* It increases the congregation's involvement in this if others beside the pastor or the leader can accompany the act of laying on of hands. Another person can accompany the man or woman who comes forward for ministry. When the individual kneels at the communion rail or sits in a chair, the other stands by and joins in the laying on of hands and perhaps the prayer. If there are Christians in the congregation who are being used in the ministry of healing, they can be invited to join in. Again, this demonstrates that what is being done is not the ministry of an individual but of the whole

Church. Forms of words used at the laying on of hands are provided in service books and manuals, but many will prefer to use spontaneous prayer. The Holy Spirit will often give to those who minister a prayer that speaks directly for the individual's condition and hopes. Hands are laid firmly but gently on the head by the pastor or leader, clasping the forehead and the back of the head as if holding a football; this avoids the heavy weight of hands pressing down on the top of the head. Others joining in place their hands on the shoulders. One asks for the gift of healing. Another follows with an act of thanksgiving. The one who is being ministered to should be encouraged to say a few words of praise to God.

Olive oil is used for anointing the sick (in Anglican and Roman Catholic denominations this oil is blessed by a bishop). The minister dips his thumb into the oil and makes the sign of the cross on the forehead with words such as, "N., *I anoint you in the name of the Father, and of the Son, and of the Holy Spirit. Amen.*" Other prayers can be added. It is handy to have a piece of cotton wool available to wipe off excess oil from the forehead.

The final hymn brings the service of prayer for healing to a close.

When such services become wellknown they tend to attract people from outside the neighbourhood. The congregation have a responsibility for contacting strangers who come forward for this ministry and keeping in touch with them afterwards. In some churches where these services are organised regularly, members of the medical profession are involved in the ministry. Many Christian doctors and nurses are still rather shy of being seen to share in the ministry of prayer with the laying on of hands, but when they do, it witnesses powerfully to the wholeness of the Church's approach to this task.

Inevitably questions are asked about the justification for these kind of services. The only answer is to see what the Lord can do through them. When people tell me that they have "intellectual problems" about the ministry of healing, I suggest to them that they set their intellectual problems on one side for a while and engage in this ministry to see what happens. And if that does not satisfy them, I point to the success of the healing ministry in some of the indigenous Churches in places like Africa. It is claimed that these Churches resort to prayer for healing because of the shortage of medical aid. This shortage is real enough, of course, but it is not the main reason for their success. Although their members believe in the power of modern medicine (and, indeed, believe in the power of traditional medicine as well), these Christians know that without faith in the God who sent Jesus Christ to proclaim the Gospel of the kingdom by healing as well as by word, any medicine is as nothing. Their therapeutic and holistic approach to disease and healing has reintegrated this ministry with the Church's mission.

A visitor in the Church of the Redeemer at Houston was standing next to a member of one of the house communities in that parish one Sunday morning during the eucharist. At one point in the service the visitor saw his neighbour lean forward and exchange a few words with a woman sitting in front of him. He saw this man lay his hands on the woman's shoulder and pray briefly. Then the woman stood up, smiled at the one who had prayed with her, and whispered something to him. The man turned to the visitor. "She's my mother-in-law," he said; "she had a spinal problem, and she's just been cured." He said this in a matter-of-fact way, as if he was passing on a piece of ordinary good news. Later in the day, the visitor saw the woman stooping as she worked all afternoon in a garden without any trace of difficulty. But no one else said anything about the change in her. They accepted the healing as something normal in their lives. Perhaps this incident gives us a clue about future developments in the ministry of healing within congregations. As local churches mature in the ways of the Holy Spirit, maybe it won't be necessary to have special services of prayer for healing. Maybe the ministry of healing will be exercised simply and widely by members of the congregation, outside as well as inside the services of that church, without any more fuss than the ministry of the choir or that of the Sunday School teachers.

12

Initiation

In their teaching and practice of Christian initiation the denominations can be divided roughly into two categories. Most Baptist and Pentecostal Churches, together with some Evangelical congregations, only administer baptism when an individual repents of his sins and confesses his faith in Jesus Christ as Lord and Saviour. In effect, this means when he is a teenager or an adult. Believer's baptism, as it is called, has strong New Testament support, for it seems that in apostolic days practically all those who were initiated into the Church had first come to personal faith. In these denominations the children of members are dedicated to God with the prayers of their family and the congregation that one day they will seek baptism after committing themselves to the Lord. For convenience we will call this kind of initiation "baptist".

In most other denominations baptism is administered in infancy and the individual is given an opportunity of confessing his personal faith in Jesus Christ when he has grown up. Anglicans and Roman Catholics see confirmation as an integral part of the initiation rites, and a baby is baptised on condition that he is brought to confirmation at a later stage. Great stress is placed on the sacramental efficacy of baptism as an ordinance commanded by Jesus Christ. The sacramental sign, it is argued, effects what it signifies, and by baptism the infant becomes, in the words of the Church of England Catechism, "a member of Christ, the child of God, and an inheritor of the kingdom of heaven". Repentance and faith come later as the child is brought up in a Christian home and taught to worship with a Christian congregation: this repentance and faith is affirmed publicly when he is brought to the bishop to be confirmed. Anglicans confirm with prayer and the laying on of hands, Roman Catholics with prayer and anointing with the laying on of hands. The practice of infant baptism can be traced back to the second century A.D. We will call this kind of initiation "catholic".

Although the lessons of the charismatic renewal are similar for both kinds of initiation, we will treat them separately in order to avoid too many qualifications and explanations in the discussion. We will take the "baptists" first.

Young people and adults who come forward for baptism often do so with a heritage of emotional or spiritual problems. Indeed, the act of conversion may be associated with a desire to overcome personal difficulties in their lives—drug addiction, immorality, an unhappy marriage, and so on. Preparation for baptism will then involve counselling and inner healing. In the early Church preparation for baptism included ministries of this kind to rescue catechumens from the evil influence of the pagan society in which they lived. The services, known as "scrutinies", were held during the weeks before the baptisms at Easter and were designed to deliver the candidates from the power of the devil (the solemn renunciation of the devil and all his works, still a feature of most baptismal liturgies, is a relic of these services). Modern society's influence is no less evil. Even the ministry of deliverance may be necessary if the candidate has been dabbling with spiritualism and the occult before his conversion. While not everyone will require prayer for healing before their baptism, we must be more alert than we often are to the possibility. It is naïve in the extreme to assume that an individual's personal problems will be solved when he confesses his faith in Jesus Christ as his Lord and Saviour and asks to be baptised. He will probably need much support from the pastor and the congregation before the victory of the cross is manifested in his life.

For this reason it is necessary to stress in teaching the converts that the cross is only victorious in our lives if we receive the Holy Spirit. This is not to detract from the centrality of the cross: rather, it is to centre on the cross in all its power and glory here and now, as the source of the experienced renewal and accomplished re-creation which the risen Lord seeks to work in us as the fruit of his sacrifice. "Christ redeemed us from the curse of the law, having become a curse for us ... that we might receive the promise of the Spirit through faith" (Galatians 3.13–34). We can so concentrate on the hopeless sinfulness of the sinner in order to exalt Christ's atoning death that repentance and conversion seem to be the *only* things that matter. But the full message of the Gospel is that Christ's redeeming grace can be effective in our lives at this present time, making us new persons in a real and discernible way, by the outpouring of his Holy Spirit. Baptism, then, is not just in water as a sign of repentance but in water and the Spirit as the beginning of a renewed existence.

Because this teaching is not always expounded fully, the faith of some of those who were converted in youth or early adulthood tends to be commemorative rather than dynamic. They draw their inspiration for being a Christian from what Jesus Christ did for them in the past rather than from what he is doing in their lives now. Asked to give their personal testimony, they dwell on that one momentous decision years ago to the exclusion of anything that might have happened to them since. It has to be admitted that certain popular hymns and choruses strengthen the impression that it is *only* because Jesus saved us at some critical point in the past when we were lost and gone astray that we have confidence in him now. The candidate for "baptist" initiation can be encouraged to look for even greater things that the Lord will do for him after he has become a member of the Church. He can be prepared to receive the Holy Spirit at his baptism, perhaps with an experience of personal release and the manifestation of new charisms. Even if he does not sense an overflowing joy at his baptism, he will almost certainly be conscious afterwards of an inner healing and peace signifying the Lord's indwelling.

It is a pity that "baptists" do not always include in their initiation rites a laying on of hands with prayer for the gift of the Holy Spirit after the candidate has been immersed in the water. There is scriptural evidence for this simple gesture, which identifies the Christian congregation through the pastor with the prayer that the Lord will meet the candidate's desire for more of the divine love and strength in his life. Sometimes the rejection of the laying on of hands is regarded as a way of opposing anything that might look like episcopal confirmation. But the charismatic movement has shown us that the laying on of hands can be an accompaniment to blessings of different kinds from God through the prayer of the congregation and that it is an error to link it solely with one element in the traditions of "catholic" initiation.

New rites for believer's baptism often do, in fact, include a laying on of hands. The Baptist Churches in England have no official service book, but E. A. Payne's and S. F. Winward's *Orders and Prayers for Church Worship* (1960) is widely used. This manual makes provision for prayer with the laying on of hands on those who have been baptised. The words with which the minister introduces this prayer are thoroughly charismatic:

> Let us pray that they (the newly-baptised), being blessed and strengthened by the Holy Spirit, may be fully equipped for their vocation and ministry as priests and servants of Jesus Christ. We also, in accepting them, commend them to your love and fellowship, and exhort you to encourage, help and build them up in the Lord.

A Baptist pastor I know tells his candidates to expect that they will experience the infilling of the Spirit whilst they are in the baptismal pool. Then, after they have confessed their faith in Jesus Christ and been immersed under the water, he lays his hands on their heads and prays for the gift of the Holy Spirit. At this point, he tells me, nearly each one feels a warmth and peace welling up within and many begin to praise God in a new tongue.

When we turn to the "catholic" type of Christian initiation, what was said in an earlier chapter about the home as a "little church" filled with the Holy Spirit is directly applicable. Parents can pray for those spiritual gifts which will equip them to show their children not just human love but also the love of God. In a house where the presence of Jesus Christ is acknowledged in the small as well as in the important matters of family life, children will begin to accept this as a normal Christian experience. Whether or not these children eventually respond in personal faith will depend on other things as well; nevertheless, an upbringing in a home open to the Holy Spirit will lay deep foundations in their lives on which a future commitment can be built. The justification for the practice of infant baptism rests on this work of the Spirit in the parents and their influence on their offspring. In an age when the confidence of parents is eroded by doubts about their ability to meet all that they are told is required of them for their children's psychological development, they discover that God is able to strengthen and guide them with what is necessary in love, wisdom and patience, so that "they may see their children Christianly and virtuously brought up, to thy

(God's) praise and honour" (*The Book of Common Prayer*, Solemnisation of Matrimony).

The place of confirmation in the rites of "catholic" initiation has been the subject of debate among theologians for most of this century. I do not propose to enter into this debate except to point out that, whatever we may feel about the ancient separation of confirmation from baptism, the charismatic renewal has given us a wider vision of what prayer with the laying on of hands for the gift of the Holy Spirit implies.

The new Roman Catholic confirmation rite, which came into use in the English-speaking world in 1976, contains some beautiful prayers for renewal in the Holy Spirit. The scriptural themes of being equipped to witness to Christ, to live in unity with one another, and to offer oneself in God's service predominate. In the introductory homily the bishop says to the candidates:

"You have already been baptised into Christ and now you will receive the power of his Spirit and the sign of the cross on your forehead. You must be witnesses before all the world to his suffering, death and resurrection; your way of life should at all times reflect the goodness of Christ. Christ gives varied gifts to his Church, and the Spirit distributes them among the members of Christ's body to build up the holy people of God in unity and love. Be active members of the Church, alive in Jesus Christ. Under the guidance of the Holy Spirit, give your lives completely to the service of all, as did Christ, who came not to be served but to serve."

The candidates reaffirm their baptismal promises in answer to the credal questions put to them by the bishop. The question on belief in the Holy Spirit has been amplified:

> *Do you believe in the Holy Spirit,*
> *the Lord, the giver of life,*
> *who came upon the apostles at Pentecost*
> *and today is given to you sacramentally in confirmation?*

The bishop then directs the congregation to pray that "our Father . . . will pour out the Holy Spirit to strengthen his sons and daughters with his gifts and anoint them to be more like Christ the Son of God". This is followed by the prayer for the sevenfold gifts of the Holy Spirit, said with hands stretched out over the candidates. The bishop (and the assisting priests, if there are any) dips his thumb into the oil of the chrism and makes the sign of the cross on the forehead of each candidate with the words, *N., be sealed with the gift of the Holy Spirit.*

At the end of the service the bishop prays for the whole congregation:

> *God our Father*
> *complete the work you have begun*
> *and keep the gifts of your Holy Spirit*
> *active in the hearts of your people.*
> *Make them ready to live his Gospel*
> *and eager to do his will.*
> *May they never be ashamed*
> *to proclaim to all the world Christ crucified,*
> *living and reigning for ever.*

A traditional Pentecostalist, hearing those words for the first time, could easily believe he was taking part in a service designed for those who were seeking baptism in the Spirit!

I am not suggesting it was the charismatic renewal among Roman Catholics that influenced the Sacred Congregation for the Sacraments and Divine Worship when they drafted this rite of confirmation. The Sacred Congregation would say, with complete justification, that the rite simply reflects in an updated form the traditional teaching of their Church. Nevertheless, as in other denominations, there is in the Roman Catholic Church a new awareness of the work of the Spirit in the Christian community; this is evident in the constitutions of the Second Vatican Council, the writings of numerous theologians, and the rapid spread of the charismatic renewal in that denomination. Pope John's prayer that the Council would prepare his Church for a "new Pentecost" is being answered in remarkable ways, and the rite of confirmation therefore reflects something more than traditional teaching; it reflects that traditional teaching re-examined in the light of the scriptures which themselves are being spiritually discerned through the Church's contemporary experience of the Holy Spirit.

Going forward for confirmation is still much of a social custom. Young people in church schools and youth organisations offer themselves with little motivation other than that their contemporaries are "being done". In the Anglican Church parents encourage their youngsters to be confirmed with the half-superstitious idea that somehow this will automatically engraft them into the Church for life (and are disappointed when that doesn't happen). Confirmation is also encouraged so that young people can receive Communion. In the retreat from Christianity in modern society this custom is dying rapidly. For this we have much to be thankful for. The real meaning of confirmation, as the completion of the rites of initiation for those who have been baptised as infants, stands out much more clearly and challengingly when those on whom the bishop lays his hands with prayer for the Holy Spirit are committing themselves personally to the Lord. The prayers quoted from the new Roman Catholic rite—which will doubtless be copied in confirmation services in other denominations—are obviously intended for those who are growing into faith through the work of the Spirit in their lives.

If confirmation is going to be administered meaningfully, its timing should be decided not by social convention but by a discernment of what God is doing in an individual. When one who has been baptised in infancy begins to reveal that God is equipping him with charisms for the building up of the Church, and when the fruit of the Spirit begins to appear in his relationships with others, then is the time to prepare him for confirmation which, as the final stage in the rites of initiation, represents in the "catholic" tradition the sign of the gift of the Spirit. In making this discernment pastors will seek the advice of those who know the candidate well—his parents, his friends in the congregation, and members of any group in the local church with which he is connected.

We should not be afraid to ask people to wait if this assessment is unfavourable. The husband of a communicant began attending confirmation classes, partly out of interest and partly out of a desire to share in something that his wife found helpful. After he had been a number of times it became apparent that he really had very little faith in Jesus Christ. Discussing this with him privately, he admitted this himself, and I suggested that he withdrew. The pressure on me against doing this was considerable. There is a convention in many parishes that to be asked to leave confirmation classes is a personal slight, and he told me afterwards that he had been hurt by my suggestion. For about two years he and his wife stayed away from church services. Then the Lord brought his wife through a family crisis in a glorious way, and shortly afterwards he called to see me. He assured me that he now had a growing faith in Jesus Christ and he asked if he could start attending confirmation classes again. After his confirmation he and his wife were baptised in the Spirit and together they entered a remarkably effective joint ministry as leaders of a house group. The earlier pruning had been a prelude to a gracious fruit.

When I prepared candidates for confirmation during my early years as a parish priest, I led them through potted courses on the Bible and Christian doctrine, employing whatever teaching aids were available—printed notes, filmstrips, visits to churches. We said one or two prayers together at each class and spent a quiet hour in church just before the confirmation service. I checked to see that they attended services regularly and I gave them an opportunity to make their first confession. But I did little to help them recognise the power of God in their lives or to experience his presence in the Christian community. Furthermore, when we rehearsed what they had to do in the confirmation service, I earnestly warned them that they would not *feel* anything when the bishop laid his hands on their heads. What mattered to me at that point was to make sure the boys had not put too much hair oil on their heads and that the girls' veils were securely fastened! I had not told them much about spiritual gifts because I was so vague on that subject myself. Looking back I see now that my great error was that, although I taught them to *repent* and to *believe*, I did nothing to encourage them to *receive*.

When I learned more from the charismatic renewal, the content and purpose of the confirmation classes changed. I still taught the Bible and Christian doctrine, but I was more concerned that the candidates should be given opportunities to experience what it means to be members of a Spirit-filled fellowship. I arranged for them to have times of sharing in discussion and prayer with others. I took them to existing prayer groups and to forms of worship that were more spontaneous and full of praise than they had encountered before. Through counselling either with me or with other members of the congregation, they were shown how to open their lives to the healing grace of God and to seek his gifts through which they could serve him. Instead of just offering them small tasks of church administration, helping to clean the sanctuary or to deliver the parish magazine (a common technique for involving new members!) I also tried to put them in positions where they would assume responsibility for the pastoral care of others. Shortly after her own confirmation one woman, a school teacher, was given the task of preparing a group of teenage girls for confirmation. She communicated to them a zeal in faith which affected all of them, and for years afterwards that group continued to keep in touch with her, even after two or three of them had temporarily lapsed from the Church.

Should confirmation candidates expect a Pentecostal experience when the bishop lays his hands on their heads? Dennis Bennett's story of how a woman began speaking in tongues when she was confirmed is wellknown. (The story goes on to say that the bishop concerned was so startled at this unexpected phenomenon that he jerked his hands away from her as if he had received an electric shock!) But we must not be misled by this. It is essential to teach that what matters in a confirmation service is that candidates should be open to receive the Holy Spirit, not that they should have dramatic experiences. If we urge candidates to try speaking in tongues when they are confirmed, their attention will be on the gift of tongues rather than the gift of the Spirit. Tongues should be explained along with the other charisms, and in a local church which is being renewed charismatically confirmation candidates will, no doubt, be familiar with it; but to isolate this spiritual gift as something special to be expected at confirmation is to throw an intolerable strain on the candidate, who will become anxious as to whether he "has it" or not. A wiser policy is to encourage candidates to pray in tongues after their confirmation in the group to which they belong. By then the Spirit's presence and power will have become evident to them in other ways and if tongues is not to be one of their charisms they need not feel disappointed.

With candidates in their 'teens and early twenties, tongues is not usually much of a problem. They have not had time to acquire the anxieties that bother older people about this gift and they embrace it with the freshness of youth. I have met many young people in charismatic prayer groups exhibiting a maturity in the spiritual life that surprised me. The gift of tongues was often the beginning of this spiritual growth. While such young people will naturally want to meet together, they should be encouraged to relate to older members of the congregation as well. Whenever I am asked to take a group of thirty or forty from a congregation for a weekend conference, I ask if places can be reserved for some of the younger Christians. The weekend together gives the younger and the older members time to get to know one another, and the contributions of the former are nearly always as valuable as the contributions of the latter.

Whatever form initiation takes—the baptism of those who have come to personal faith in the "baptist" tradition, or the baptism in infancy followed by confirmation and first Communion in the "catholic" tradition—the Pentecostal experience which is called baptism in the Spirit has to be seen in relationship to it. Otherwise baptism in the Spirit becomes a "second blessing", and most of us in the mainline denominations find this concept difficult to accept. In the scriptures and in the traditional theologies of initiation there is plenty of room for the idea of later spiritual growth emerging out of initiation into the Christian fellowship; there is not much room for the teaching of a two-stage means of entry into that fellowship (however much confirmation may appear to indicate that in the "catholic" tradition). So in as much as baptism in the Spirit results in a greater love for God and for one another, it represents a fuller appropriation by the individual of what God offers him through initiation. Through this experience—whether it is dramatic or gradual—we become in reality what we are sacramentally, beloved by the Lord, chosen by God from the beginning to be saved, through sanctification by the Spirit and belief in the truth.

In both kinds of Christian initiation, sponsorship is usually provided for the candidates—godparents for those who are baptised in infancy, and sponsors for those seeking believer's baptism. There is much to be said for a member of a charismatic prayer group acting as one of the sponsors, if it is possible to arrange this. In the case of teenagers and adults (and confirmation candidates can be offered a sponsor as part of their preparation if the spiritual support from their homes is lacking, as well as candidates for believer's baptism) the sponsor is then able to introduce the candidate to the group as a more personal form of the Christian fellowship into which he is being fully initiated. Unfortunately it is not always possible to arrange these things in a tidy and easy way. But it is worthwhile making the attempt. Where a number of candidates prepare together, it is sometimes possible for the pastor to continue their meetings after their baptism or confirmation so that they develop their own corporate life as a prayer group. In time the pastor slowly disengages himself from it and hands over the leadership to a suitable member.

Theologians and liturgists of the "catholic" tradition dream of the day when every new Christian will be led through repentance and faith to the receiving of the Spirit in one glorious, trans-figuring experience. Then the theology of Christian initiation would be demonstrated in its living truth. Then the liturgy of baptism, confirmation and first Communion would be an out-ward expression of an inner reality; sacramental grace and per-sonal experience would be perfectly married. But our rela-tionships with God are not controlled by theologians and litur-gists! Our spiritual pilgrimage is usually episodic—and unex-pected. We turn to God, we reach up to him, we hesitate, we doubt, we stumble into sin, we persist in disobedience, we repent, we are forgiven, we start again—and so we go on, hesitantly, fearfully, sometimes despairingly, sometimes hopefully, slowly becoming aware that it is Christ within who is leading us. The rites of initiation proclaim what God has done for us in Jesus Christ and what he longs to do for us, but our response in the Holy Spirit takes more than our human lifespan to perfect.

13

Ecumenism

I attended one of the first charismatic meetings in Belfast shortly after the fresh outbreak of the troubles in the early 'seventies. Over a long weekend about one hundred and fifty people came together for a series of gatherings which culminated in a eucharist celebrated in the Church of the Resurrection, the modern building serving the Church of Ireland chaplaincy in the Queen's University. The men and women who attended came from the Irish Republic as well as from Northern Ireland. A group of Roman Catholics—Jesuits, nuns, seminarians and lay folk—travelled up from Dublin specially for the occasion. When he gave his testimony, a Jesuit priest confessed that he had never crossed the Border before in his life. He had studied in Rome and visited different parts of the world, but he had been too scared to travel into that part of Ireland that represented Protestant power for him. He admitted that when the train carrying him to Belfast crossed into Northern Ireland that Friday afternoon, a feeling of terror had gripped him. It was not until he was warmly embraced in Belfast station by a group of people whom he had never met before that he realised he was among friends—friends who, during the weekend, he came to recognise as brothers and sisters in Jesus Christ.

The weekend culminated in an ecumenical eucharist in the church on the Sunday evening. For the giving of the Peace and the receiving of the sacrament, we formed a large circle round the free-standing altar. As I looked round during the singing of *We are one in the Spirit, we are one in the Lord*, I recognised members of different denominations—Anglicans, Baptists, Methodists, Presbyterians, Roman Catholics . . .

It was a moving experience. We were near to weeping for joy. In the midst of the grim signs of terrorism in Belfast—the ruined buildings, the broken and boarded houses, the barriers, the security forces, the armoured cars and the so-called "Peace Line"—here were representatives of the bitter religious divisions in Ireland discovering a deep unity of love within a celebration of God's redeeming work in Jesus Christ.

The ecumenical significance of the charismatic renewal is difficult to overestimate. Longing for more of the love of Jesus Christ in their lives, members of different denominations have found themselves drawn more towards one another. The Pentecostal experience shared by Christians across the traditional boundaries is endowing the search for unity with a power and an urgency that it has not known before. So often ecumenism (especially in local churches) has had an ulterior motive: economy in the sharing of a building, sticking together in the midst of an increasingly indifferent world, undertaking various projects in order to spread diminishing resources over a wider area. Renewal in the Spirit brings ordinary Christians who do not belong to joint committees and theological commissions to the prime reason for unity: the oneness of God as revealed in Jesus Christ through the Holy Spirit. *Ut unum sint*: the prayer of Christ becomes the prayer of his disciples as, by the one Spirit, they are caught up into his petition to his Father and their Father.

Although we live in what will certainly be called by future church histories "the ecumenical century", the experience of a real spiritual unity among Christians of different denominations has been confined to a comparative few at grassroots level. Those who have come together for any period of time through the World Council of Churches or through national councils have sometimes discovered this spiritual unity among themselves. Behind documents like the *Agreed Statements* of the Anglican-Roman Catholic International Commission (1971–76) and the publication *One Baptism, One Eucharist and a Mutually Recognised Ministry* (Faith and Order Paper No. 73, World Council of Churches, 1975) are relationships between individuals and groups representing various Churches which go further than friendly links formed by common interests and tasks.

But in congregations this is rare. In spite of all that councils of churches have done in cities and towns encouraging joint services, united walks of witness, exchange of pulpits and ecumenical study groups, unity has been found in practical projects such as

Christian Aid collections or joint ventures of a charitable nature rather than in experiences of the oneness of God through his Word and his action. What has been lacking is committed, costly fellowship and prayer. The Weeks of Prayer for Christian Unity organised in January each year by the World Council of Churches and the Roman Catholic Secretariat for Promoting Christian Unity have often produced little more than a gesture towards local ecumenism. Indeed, I do not think that it is an exaggeration to say that the Unity Octave has been counterproductive in some places. Having come together for a joint service with Christians of other traditions, congregations and their pastors have comforted themselves with the thought that they have "done the unity thing" for another year, heaved a sigh of relief, and busied themselves with their own concerns for the next fifty-one weeks.

Furthermore, where ecumenical projects are initiated, the oneness of the Spirit that is so often talked about proves to be strangely elusive. In England there are about three hundred local ecumenical projects—pastoral schemes varying from shared building agreements to joint clergy teams—set up officially by the denominations. Yet in spite of all the goodwill that went into their formation, the congregations who have come together within them have experienced considerable difficulty in finding that unity they had hoped for before the project was launched. They have cooperated in an attitude of tolerant coexistence rather than in a spirit of growing commitment to one another in Christ. What they have achieved together seems to have been inspired on an unspoken, mutual understanding that each will limit themselves to carefully defined areas.

Lack of real spiritual unity has been the indirect cause of a casual kind of ecumenism that has little meaning. It is a social rather than a religious phenomenon. Individuals have found good friends in other denominations and changed their allegiances for no other reason than wanting to be together. Marriages between Christians of different traditions are commonplace without the personal difficulties that they once created among the families concerned. Disunity is to do with outdated quarrels, it is said. Let the dead bury their dead. The past is no concern of ours. It is the future that matters. Inasmuch as this attitude indicates a decline of religious intolerance, it is to be welcomed. But the indifference that goes with it is saddening. There is no positive desire to encourage Christians to come together in a Christ-centred way. Many of the things that caused schisms and divisions in the Body of Christ are best forgotten, but there are other things that should be our concern. For at its centre the cause of disunity is the result of our responding to God's Word in different ways and mis-understanding and mistrusting one another in the process. Con-sequently, we are all the losers—we miss the spiritual gifts that God is bestowing on others. The ecumenical movement is the Spirit's impulse in Christians to repent and rediscover Jesus Christ in one another.

Because its chief message is obedience to the Spirit of God, the charismatic movement has brought to ecumenism the spiritual dynamic that has so often been lacking in local neighbourhoods. Usually this influence begins at the meetings which I have already described when Christians from different congregations in an area assemble for a time of prayer and praise. In England many of these meetings were initiated by the Fountain Trust and they have continued in various cities and towns under the direction of core groups formed by pastors and laity from neighbouring con-gregations. They were given a special impetus in the seventies by the Fountain Trust's *Glory in the Church* weekends and by the celebration of *Come Together* and *If My People*, specially scripted and prepared acts of worship with a highly charismatic flavour. Events like these brought together hundreds across their denominational boundaries. The meetings organised by the Catholic Charismatic Renewal Committees in the United States pulled in tens of thousands from different denominations.

Since the numbers at these meetings are so large, the rela-tionships between those who attend are obviously slight. Nevertheless, they are occasions when prejudices are erased and misunderstandings corrected. At these meetings there is great emphasis on praising God, and this means that those who come are encouraged to look at the Lord first rather than at the things that divide them—an exercise which, in itself, has proved to be a powerful means of healing Christian disunity. This is in marked contrast to the atmosphere of the united services organised during the Week of Prayer for Christian Unity, when the tendency is to make the service a devotional interlude before the main event—a speaker explaining the differences between the Churches!

There are other encounters across the denominational barriers at charismatic meetings. Evangelicals hear the scriptures read and expounded inspiringly by churchmen whom they had previously regarded as doctrinally unsound; Roman Catholics experience a Spirit-led ministry from one who is neither Catholic, male nor ordained! (This last note was prompted by an incident at a Roman Catholic charismatic meeting: after Margaret, my wife, had spoken briefly she was surrounded by appreciative listeners who told her how refreshing it had been to hear a woman addressing them within the context of an act of worship for the first time!) In the various forms of group prayer and ministry that are a feature of these assemblies individuals from one denomination experience the Spirit of Christ in those of other Christian traditions.

This is followed up in residential conferences and teaching weekends. Again, they provide for Christians from different traditions to share in a close fellowship, to be drawn by a common interest to be more open to God in their lives and to discover a unity of the Spirit among themselves. I have taken part in many of these, and I can say that nearly every time I have not noticed the denominational allegiance of those who are there. Sometimes I have made guesses—and been wrong. At one conference I was quite convinced that in a discussion group a man with strong views about adult baptism must be a strict Baptist, only to discover later that he had been brought up as a Roman Catholic and remained one all his life.

To say that individuals are "converted" to ecumenism (in the deepest sense of that word) through charismatic encounters is not an exaggeration. The famous hymn to the Holy Spirit runs, "What is rigid gently bend". Rigidity in dogmatic traditions is certainly bent in these circumstances—and not always so gently! A man who is a committed Evangelical was taken to a "charismatic mass" in a Roman Catholic convent one evening. He would hardly have gone there out of curiosity: he went because the preacher was a famous Pentecostal speaker and this was the only opportunity he had of hearing him. To his embarrassment he was shown to a seat on the front row where he had a full view of everything and was himself in full view of everybody. The following day he could hardly speak to me as he recalled his delighted surprise. It wasn't the sermon that he remembered but the service and the people who took part in it. The priest had conducted it, he said, with a freedom, sincerity and joy that the

Evangelical had never experienced in his own church. He had been greeted and prayed for by the Catholics around him with a love that overwhelmed him. He was invited to receive the sacrament with the rest. "I tell you," he exclaimed eagerly, "they were born-again Christians—those students and the rest! And as for the nuns—well, I've never met women who loved Jesus more! You could see their love shining in their faces." He had been "converted".

But bonds of real union are formed most strongly in the small groups. As a few people come together weekly or fortnightly in ordinary homes, vicarages, clergy-houses, manses, convents and colleges for Bible study and prayer, they grow (if the group is properly led and supported) into spiritual families that transcend denominational differences. This is perhaps the most important place where the charismatic renewal is building bridges between the Churches. In these face-to-face situations Christians experience how much they can learn from one another and how much they can help one another through their oneness in Christ, in spite of the differences that continue between their denominations. A Methodist may enter into a personal experience of renewal after prayer and the laying on of hands by a Roman Catholic. An Anglican priest may receive a gift of healing through the ministry of a man and his wife who are Baptists. It is not difficult to imagine what the effect of experiences like these are likely to be on the ecumenical outlook of those who are blessed through them.

Charismatics who get involved in ecumenical groups of this type are sometimes afraid to discuss the doctrinal and historical problems that divide their denominations for fear that they might spoil the new-found spirit of unity in the group. What are the others to do if the Roman Catholic members offer prayers to the Blessed Virgin Mary and to the saints? What should those who are willing to approach the scriptures aided by the tools of contemporary biblical criticism say if someone interprets texts from a fundamentalist standpoint? And how are they all to approach those issues which find Christians in different camps—remarriage in church after divorce, birth control, abortion and euthanasia, violence and non-violence, and so on?

Earlier in this book I have described how groups grow together in the Spirit by learning to listen to one another and to trust one another in spite of personal differences. The same process will take place in an ecumenical group, if members are prepared to wait until they are ready to face with the grace of God the strains and tensions that differences between them will bring. But the members must first have an opportunity to realise their spiritual unity, and this takes time. They should not try to force a discussion on divisive issues but allow the topics to arise naturally through their meetings. Under those who are guiding the group it will be possible for members to look at these difficult matters and gradually learn from one another how each understands his or her ideas as a response to the Word of God. There must be no attempt to argue someone out of his opinion. Rather, testing the differences against the scriptures and against the traditional teachings of the Church, they should always go back to the basic question, What is the Lord saying to us through our differences? It will be a painful, exasperating undertaking; it will strain relationships to what appears to be an unspiritual breaking-point; but when the group has come through it, they will have learned together more of what it means to hear the Word of God today.

There are some who accuse charismatics of clouding doctrinal issues among Christians in their search for spiritual experiences. They point out that there must be unity in truth as well as unity in spirit. The Holy Spirit has not been absent from the Church, they say, when he led her through her teachings and disciplines in the past, and we must not ignore what God has said to us through our traditions—in spite of the divisions they have sometimes created. The accusation is not entirely fair—as I hope the approach to the matter of doctrinal divisions in this chapter has shown—but it must nevertheless be faced. Certainly there is a tendency for some charismatic ecumenical groups to brush aside controversial opinions and talk only about the unity they are experiencing. This tendency is dangerous because it robs their encounter of a reality—the reality of the differences that still exist between them and the denominations they represent. There is no lack of theological reflection on the charismatic experience associated with the Pentecostal renewal and we should not be shy of applying that reflection to the divided state in which Christians find themselves.

But in the end we will have to answer the accusation by saying that the search for doctrinal purity among Christians has never been completely successful because God's revelation of himself to man in Jesus Christ cannot be captured for ever within the terms of theological statements. The truth spoken of in the New Testament is the person of Jesus Christ, his coming into the world, his good news and mighty works, his death, his resurrection and his ascension, not a set of propositions about God which we have to accept without question. The promise contained in the fourth Gospel is that the Holy Spirit would lead us into all truth, not that the day would come in this life when we had arrived at all truth. How we are led in that voyage of discovery will depend on the effect our personal experience of God has on our lives. And it is experience of God that the charismatic movement is helping us to discern and to test. Believing can never be just an intellectual assent to Christian teaching—texts from the scriptures, creeds, catechisms, theological definitions, rites and sermons. It must be corroborated by our present experience of what God is saying to us and doing in and through us *now*.

This experience of God will come to us first of all through what belongs to our past and that of the denomination of which we are members. The way our parents, our Christian relatives, our early pastors, teachers and companions responded to God in their lives will influence us; and this response will in its turn have been influenced by the way the Holy Spirit has led our forefathers in the faith to understand the scriptures, to preach the Gospel, to worship and to order their lives and that of the denomination. All these influences will merge to make the traditions which we have received as Anglicans, Baptists, Methodists and so on. Yet our experience of God will not be limited by those traditions. We shall hear the Lord speaking to us through our contemporaries, and especially through those who belong to other traditions. There will be apparent conflicts and real confusion: the initial result of growing into unity is chaos, but it is a chaos over which the Holy Spirit broods. In time he leads us to a greater vision of God as our faith, hope and love mature in the encounter with others, and he will glorify Jesus Christ even more in our lives.

We can therefore refute the accusation that the charismatic renewal clouds doctrinal issues in the ecumenical scene. Rather we can point out that the charismatic renewal raises new questions and necessitates a theological re-think. All spiritual renewals in the Church's history, including Pentecostalism, call on theologians to exercise their particular charisms in the service of their fellow Christians to help the Church understand and be obedient to what God is saying and doing through those renewals. To do this theologians themselves must be open to the Spirit and united to God in Jesus Christ. It is not their task to tell the Church what its future is to be: still less is it to pronounce on what it is possible and what it is impossible for God to do! Their responsibility is to examine the presuppositions behind all the accounts, the explanations and the prophecies which arise from the charismatic renewal and to uncover the theology that is implicit in those experiences.

To follow God's call to unity is to experience from time to time the strain of loyalty to our own denomination. What the Lord is saying to us in our ecumenical groups does not always seem to be in harmony with what he is saying to us through our traditions and local congregation. We feel torn in two directions. We have already discussed this tension in the matter of the relationships between those who have been baptised in the Holy Spirit and their local church. The difference in this case is that the tension is more complex—towards our own denomination, towards the group, towards certain individuals in it who represent other denominations. The right response to this tension is to recognise in its pain the sufferings of Christ's body in disunity, and in its lesson the wideness of God's mercy and the mystery of his purposes. While other Christians still reflect in their lives the love of God, we cannot allow ourselves to be separated from them. The differences between us mean that we have to go on helping one another to be more obedient to Jesus Christ. Then we shall find that we can be even more loyal to our own traditions for we shall appreciate more deeply what is truly of the Lord in them.

Peter Hocken, a Roman Catholic priest, has expressed this well: "Ecumenism means that no Church can adequately define itself by exclusion, and that each tradition needs to keep redefining itself by increasing inclusion. This 'confusion of the Spirit' is the very opposite of indifferentism, the essence of which is that traditions and denominations do not matter; on the contrary, ecumenism means that all traditions matter, old and new. Dual or multiple allegiance is not a diminution in attachment to one's own Church, but the acquisition of additional loyalties that enrich and deepen the original attachment."*

* *New Heaven? New Earth?* by Simon Tugwell, Peter Hocken, George Every, John Orme Mills (Darton, Longman and Todd, 1976) p. 50.

To go back to that ecumenical eucharist in Belfast that I described at the beginning of this chapter. I have no doubt that there were many present in that circle of worshippers who were experiencing a tension between their sense of loyalty to their denomination and their feeling that what they should do in the Church of the Resurrection was to express their unity with one another in the sincerest possible way. The Presbyterians and Baptists must have felt torn between rejecting the things that Roman Catholicism stood for and entering into a spiritual unity with the Roman Catholics they had met. The Roman Catholics must have been conscious that in receiving Communion at a eucharist presided over by an Anglican they were breaking the rule about intercommunion in their denomination. But I do not believe that any Christian in that church could have said that these Protestants and Catholics were being disobedient to God. For in the heart of a city which stands in the modern world as a symbol of the hatred that centuries of religious controversy can generate, we were moved by the Holy Spirit to receive the sacrament of unity together as a prophetic act pointing to God's ultimate will for his people.

How a congregation moves into closer relationships with other congregations of different denominations in a locality is a problem which can only be solved by those who undertake that task. Circumstances will vary from one neighbourhood to another. The opportunities will differ—a shared church building here, a joint team ministry there. But always there must be two objectives in those congregations who seek to come together, so that they do this with their gaze on the Lord and his will rather than on each other.

First, to worship him together. That worship is not to be just a formal act lasting one hour arranged occasionally for those who happen to be free, but an accepted discipline of praying to seek his will and to praise him in small groups as well as in larger gatherings. When I am invited to address an ecumenical meeting on a topic, I nearly always ask if a portion of the time can be devoted to worship—the spontaneous, praise-filled prayer that I have experienced in charismatic circles. And nearly always the people afterwards have thanked me, not for my talk, but for leading them in prayer. It has been the worship that has given them a deeper sense of their oneness in Jesus Christ.

Secondly, to proclaim the Gospel of the kingdom together. There are many ways in which the Lord leads his people into a fuller participation in his mission in the world, and it is in sharing in his mission that we are drawn closer to one another. As long as we just go on looking at one another we shall only be aware of our differences. One congregation will be jealous of its traditions, the other will be fearful of losing its possessions (a church building, the parish endowments). But when we engage in the Lord's mission together, then we begin to see Jesus at work in one another and to draw strength and inspiration from one another through the different gifts that his Spirit bestows upon us. To see the differences between our congregation and the one next door in terms of the manifold charisms given to equip the whole Church for its upbuilding, is to see those differences from the perspective of God's grace rather than from that of man's disobedience. Then can we discern what has to be rejected as we grow together and what has to be renewed.

The practical application of these two objectives is the main agenda for any local council of churches. Many such councils are realising this. They are less concerned with maintaining an ecumenical programme of joint activities; they see their function as one of enabling people from different denominations in a neighbourhood to relate to one another as the Spirit leads them. Among them there grows up at least one group that accepts as its vocation the ministry of prayer and waiting on God on behalf of the congregations. The great leaders of the ecumenical movement have been insisting that unity will emerge among the denominations when Christians pray together, and local councils of churches are discovering this. The charismatic prayer group offers them a model of how such a group can come together.

But as well as one or more prayer groups, a local council of churches requires at least one person—perhaps a chairman or a secretary—who, in close association with the clergy, can move freely among the member-congregations. He visits different churches in turn and meets their officers and committees. He becomes the ecumenical figure in the neighbourhood, representing the desire of the churches to grow together and keeping open the lines of communication between them. Such an individual obviously needs a wide understanding of and sensitivity towards the differences between the denominations in order to operate in this way with the trust of all. In fact, he needs a special gift of the Spirit, for in his ministry he is fulfilling a prophetic role—pointing the churches forward to their common destiny in Jesus Christ. And the charismatic renewal is teaching us things about that kind of special gift, too.

14

House Churches

The A225 leaves the main road from London to Maidstone just beyond the village of Farningham in Kent. Driving southwards we enter the next village, Eynsford. Opposite the church we turn into a lane and cross over an old bridge (or splash through the ford beside the bridge if the river Darenth is low enough) and continue for about one mile towards Lullingstone. Off this lane are the excavations of a large Roman villa. We park our car, pay the entrance fee, and view the archaeological remains now protected by a huge shed. The walkway enables us to look down on the foundations of the villa and to admire the fine Bellerophon mosaic in the pavement of the apsed *triclinum*. It is one of the artistic treasures of the Roman period in Britain. The mosaic is intact except where a plough once scored its surface years before anyone knew the villa existed (it was not properly excavated until after the Second World War).

But what interests us most among these remains are the foundations of the three small rooms at the northern end of the villa. The plaster of these rooms was once decorated with six figures, three of whom at least were in the *Orans* attitude (that is, like charismatics at a prayer meeting with their arms outstretched), and with *Chi-Rho* signs (the monogram made up of the initial letters of the words "Christ Reigns" in Greek). From this evidence scholars are fairly confident that these rooms were once used for Christian worship.

Sometime in the middle of the fourth century the owner of the villa and his family became Christians. The busts of the ancestral gods were unceremoniously stacked in the cellar and the rooms set aside as a chapel. A door was made so that people could enter the chapel without having to go through the interior of the villa. Archaeologists believe that a Christian congregation continued to use these rooms for worship well into the fifth century after the rest of the villa had been left empty. Eventually the whole building was destroyed by fire and nothing is known of what happened to that group of believers. The Lullingstone villa, then, contains the remains of one of the earliest known house churches in Britain. A congregation assembled there at least two hundred years before 597 A.D. when Augustine and his monks landed in Kent to begin the evangelisation of the south of England. The excavations put us in touch with Christians who did not know what it was to worship in a church building.

After they were debarred from the temple in Jerusalem and the synagogues of the dispersion, the followers of Jesus Christ met in one another's homes for fellowship, for instruction and for worship (unless they were able to meet out-of-doors, like Lydia and her companions at Philippi, or to assemble in a hired hall, as Paul and his friends did in Ephesus). Some of the apostle's letters are addressed to the Church at the house of one or more of its members—Prisca and Aquila, Nympha and Philemon (Romans 16.5, I Corinthians 16.19, Colossians 4.15, Philemon 2). The Acts of the Apostles gives us snapshots of congregations meeting in homes for the celebration of the eucharist and to hear a visiting speaker (2.46, 20.20). The Christians who crowded into those small rooms in the villa at Lullingstone were following a tradition that was as old as the faith they professed.

If the congregation that met in those rooms had survived and flourished, they would have outgrown their place of assembly and had to provide something larger. Some of the churches in Rome are examples of this kind of growth. If we visit S. Clemente we can go down into the crypt of the present church and find ourselves in what is virtually the remains of a fifth century church which it has replaced. Below this crypt are other remains, those of rooms in a house that was once used for worship, together with a tiny temple of Mithras. These rooms may well have been the home of a Christian family as early as the time when Peter and Paul came to the city. (It has been suggested that the dedication of this church goes back to the Clement whom Paul mentioned in Galatians 4.3, but this is almost certainly a piece of romantic fiction. It is likely, however, that the name of the Christian family was Clement, and that this name stuck to become the dedication title of the church that was built over their old home. The family may have donated the property to the congregation as a site for a church.) So archaeology has here revealed how a congregation developed from a house church to a parish church, which has persisted into modern times. A story very different from that of the little congregation meeting in a villa in Kent in faraway Britannia!

This scriptural and historical background should be remembered in the current debate about house churches. Although house churches as such are not associated only with the charismatic movement, the subject often comes up in discussions about renewal. Usually in this debate the house church and the local church are treated as if they are opponents of one another. The assumption is made that there is no room in a neighbourhood for both kinds of Christian gathering. The background I have sketched at least suggests that this assumption might be a false one. If we remember the essential nature of the Church, we shall see that a congregation is created by people, not by buildings; and if we recall the complex nature of modern society, we shall see that geographical considerations are no longer relevant. There is no reason why both kinds of churches should not exist side-by-side in a neighbourhood, just as the different denominations do. Problems of unity are not necessarily solved by having one place of worship in an area. There will always be a need for smaller, separate meeting-places for Christian groups in society, especially if their fellowship is to be strengthened in the ways we have already discussed.

This has been the pattern since the construction of the first church buildings in Christendom. Although countries like Britain were eventually divided into parishes, legal areas assigned to the clergy and congregation of a single church, other congregations continued to meet in houses and other establishments. The monastery had its own chapel. So did the castle of the early middle ages and the great house of the renaissance period. Schools, colleges and hospitals have nearly always had their own rooms for worship (some of those rooms developed into buildings like King's College Chapel, Cambridge!) The different kinds of congregations worshipped in their own churches or chapels for centuries without any thought of division (except where rivalries in ecclesiastical jurisdiction between bishop and abbot or pope and monarch created tensions between the two). From a pastoral point of view it is never considered odd that certain social groups should worship separately today—boys and girls in a school chapel, staff and students in a college chapel, and nurses and patients in a hospital chapel. Why, then, does the emergence of a house church in a neighbourhood rouse fears in some of our contemporaries?

These fears may be part of our religious inheritance. From the time of the Reformation attendance at one's own parish church was regarded as a mark of loyalty, not only to the established Church but also to the Crown. This was especially the case in England where the fortunes of both were closely bound up together in Tudor and Stuart eras. To be anything other than a member of the Church of England was to be a quisling. That is why Roman Catholic priests had to say mass secretly in the homes of those who adhered to the old faith. That is why the Conventicle Act of 1664 made it illegal for anyone over the age of sixteen to attend any "assembly, conventicle, or meeting, under colour or pretence of any exercise of religion, in other manner than according to the liturgy and practice of the Church of England". The Act of Toleration eased this persecution of non-Anglicans, but from those days there has lingered a suspicion of Christians who gather for worship outside the official structures—a suspicion which is also found nowadays among those whose descendants once met in house church situations, Roman Catholics and members of the Free Churches in England.

Some of the house churches flourishing today have set themselves in open opposition to the established denominations. They claim that the institutional denominations can no longer offer members an authentic Christian fellowship and their message to charismatics and others is, "Come out from among them." The exclusiveness of some of these house churches also makes them intolerant of congregations which attempt to be more comprehensive in their membership. Such an attitude is, to say the least, unhelpful and uncharitable, but it should not prevent us from recognising that the house church has a communal strength which contrasts sharply with the communal weakness of many local congregations. I can illustrate this by describing a house church that I visited in 1975.

The house church met in an older semi-detached on Spring Hill, Tavistock. Several cars were parked in the drive and along the road outside the house when I arrived at ten o'clock one Sunday morning. Some children were playing in the garden. In the dining-room a group of people stood about drinking coffee and chatting. Colin Bond, the leader, in whose house the meeting was held, introduced us. He told us that the group had been coming together regularly on Sundays for two years.

At half-past-ten the twenty-five or so adults moved into the large sitting-room while the children were taken down into the furnished basement for their own activities. We sat in a circle for a short period of prayer and praise, and then we had what was virtually a business session. Four members talked about the visits they made occasionally to a prison. Someone reported that two members were ill and arrangements were made to visit them. Colin announced that an ecumenical event was to take place in the parish church later that week.

One of the young men belonging to the group was to be married in the near future and an old policeman's helmet had been used to collect an offering for him to assist him in putting the deposit on a house. Just over two hundred pounds had been raised in this way from the group. The treasurer briefly presented the accounts. I learned that considerable sums had been given to missions and that the group had assisted an Anglican ordinand with a family to meet his expenses the previous Christmas. The standard of giving was high. As far as I could judge, most of the members of the house group tithed their income for it. Colin was planning to give up his job as a school-master and commit himself full-time to his ministry among them.

The children now came into the room and demonstrated what they had learned with a mime and a dance. We sang more choruses together, and then the children withdrew to play whilst we moved into worship with hymns, scripture readings, an address (followed by a short discussion) and prayers.

Lunch was served in the basement, which had a door opening into the garden. Everyone had brought food, and this was piled on a large table from which we helped ourselves, sitting in the house or in the garden. I gathered that the house church also had a weekly Bible study for some of its members on Monday evenings and a youth club on Fridays. Most of us went in cars to the sea that afternoon. The prison visitors left to fulfil their mission, and calls were made on the sick members. A few went home. That evening some went to a church in Plymouth to hear a guest speaker.

Several things impressed me about that house church.

(1) The members seemed to be more committed to one another than many in the congregations I have known. They were like an extended family. The sharing of food at lunch was only a small sign of a greater sharing with one another—like the help that was offered to one member to put a deposit on a house (a thing that might well happen in the closest of natural families).

(2) The fellowship of the house church was strong enough for members to give up most of Sunday to it. True, not all of them came every week, but the proportion of attendances was high. Since they were together for several hours each week, they had time to make decisions in common. A core group met for short business sessions, but much of the house church's activities took place within the framework of the Sunday fellowship. The day slipped easily from social chat, business, attention to children, worship, instruction, discussion, eating, going out—giving the day an integrated wholeness so that it was not easy to say that one activity was more "sacred" than another. In the parishes where I have served as curate and vicar, we would have needed different committees and groups to arrange these things for the congregation!

(3) The resources of the house church were not absorbed by the need to maintain buildings. It was fortunate for them that Colin and Joy Bond had a house that was well suited to members' needs (the Bonds would have said that their home was a gift from God for this purpose). Members had no desire for a "proper church" (the phrase I often heard from an Anglican congregation that worshipped in a dual-purpose building!). Their interest was focussed on their coming together, not on the place where that happened. They would not have been able to help their young member put a deposit on a house, or have given away such large sums of money, if they had had to raise funds to re-roof a medieval church or repair a decrepit organ.

(4) The contribution of the house church to local churches in the neighbourhood was considerable. They were known and respected over a wide area. Several who had joined the house church for a year or so had gone back to their former congregations with a deeper faith and a clearer vision of what it means to minister to others in the power of the Spirit. As far as I could tell, they avoided creating the impression that they were an exclusive group.

(5) The way the pastoral leadership of that house church had emerged was interesting. Colin and his wife had started a youth meeting in their home as a missionary project from their own congregation. Gradually this meeting had expanded to include the parents of the young people and many were converted. Colin had tried to send the converts to other local churches but had failed: they had wanted to worship together with him where they had first met and found Jesus Christ. It was only with reluctance that Colin and his wife had initiated the Sunday fellowship. Although Colin had not been ordained by a denomination, his gifts were recognised by the clergy of other local churches and they invited him to join them in various activities as a fellow pastor.

To make my description as fair as possible, however, I should add that during my visit I thought I detected certain weaknesses in this house church. The worship was rather thin, lacking the richness of the Church's liturgical traditions. During the discussions I sensed that Colin's position as leader could have been threatened by one or two other dominant personalities. And—although this was purely guesswork on my part—I suspected that it would not have been impossible for eccentricities to have established themselves among the group. These are, in fact, the perils to which most house churches are exposed. If groups are cut off from the worshipping life of the denominations, they lose much of their traditional liturgy and spirituality. Pastors of independent congregations miss the support of the wider Christian fellowship if there are no other ministers to whom they can turn. And independents are noted for adopting excessive standards for their members or over-stressing some aspect of scriptural teaching.

I know of one group of house churches where the discipline has become excessively rigorous over the course of a number of years. Each member has to solemnly vow that he or she will be submissive to the pastor, even to the extent of accepting his authority over that of a parent or a spouse. New members have to sign a document promising that they will donate a tithe of their gross pay to the house church—and they are excommunicated if they fail to keep this up. Strange doctrines are propagated, usually in the matter of the second advent of Jesus Christ and the day of judgement. Where the worst forms of sectarianism penetrate the house churches, the criticisms that have been levelled against them are completely justified.

Some house churches have a remarkable outreach. The Victoria Park Fellowship in Manchester is based on four houses in a terrace where three couples and a dozen single people live as a community, but their membership has grown in recent years as people have come to join their worship and meetings from a wide area. Various house groups have been formed among their members in different parts of Manchester, and some of their members have gone out to serve the Lord overseas. Although the Fellowship would not wish to be regarded as anything other than part of the wider Church in Manchester, its influence is comparable with that of a smaller denomination. At the time of writing there are two elders, a number of deacons, and a group of younger men who are accepting responsibilities as leaders in various aspects of the Fellowship's ministry.

If some house churches have become exclusive, those in local congregations in the neighbourhood have to ask themselves how far the attitudes of the denominations have created this situation. A pastor who finds a house church in his area has much to offer its members if he is prepared to approach them in a spirit of Christian love and accept the early suspicions and rebuffs. A house church needs the wider fellowship and apostolic ministry that he represents. It is significant that about two hundred house churches in southern England rely on the support of a number of itinerant clergy who visit them and exercise an unofficial oversight among them. A hopeful sign has recently emerged from another group of house churches. They postponed their own meetings for a period and encouraged their members to become involved in neighbouring congregations—not because their own meetings were losing their impetus, but because it was felt that the Lord was leading them to share what they had with Christians in other churches.

Those of us who are committed to the more traditional local churches can learn much about what it means to belong to a Christian community from the house churches. When we remember what the upkeep and repair of a church building involves us in, we might well pause for a moment and ask ourselves how far our life-style as a congregation is shaped by our "plant" and how far it is shaped by New Testament principles of brotherly fellowship. Does the kind of gathering for which church buildings were provided in earlier centuries create that brotherly fellowship or hinder it? Is a weekly assembly of one or two hundred people for an hour on a Sunday morning or evening the best way of expressing that brotherly fellowship in a neighbourhood? I'm not suggesting that there are simple answers to these questions, for we can neither cut ourselves off completely from our past nor can we take one form of Christian community today and say that it is to be normative for everyone. My plea is that we should be aware of hidden assumptions and inherited prejudices and that we should discern what the Lord is saying to us through the house church movement. And we shall do this when we see them in the perspective which I have briefly outlined and realise that the local church and the house church are essentially one—a gathering of God's people in the name of Jesus Christ.

In a recent letter to me Colin Bond said that the numbers coming to the meetings on Sundays had increased so much that he and his friends now met in a school hall. At about the same time I read a report by a Church of England archdeacon on the needs and resources of his diocese in which he said that, with the rising cost of fuel for heating church buildings, several congregations were now gathering for their services either in the vestry of their church or a suitable room in the rectory, at least during the winter months. And my mind went back to the Christian rooms in the villa at Lullingstone and the church of S. Clemente built over the home of some early Christian Roman citizen . . .

15
Communities

The growth of small communities of Christians living together or sharing closely in each others' lives has been a striking development in England, North America and other parts of the Western world during the past ten years. Although not all these communities draw their inspiration from the charismatic renewal, many of them come together when, following a Pentecostal experience of release and growth in the Holy Spirit, individuals and families feel an impulse to join with others in community living. Often they are ecumenical in character—Christians of different denominations discovering a unity in the Spirit in spite of the things that have traditionally separated them.

There is no set pattern or lifestyle for these communities. They vary in size from several hundreds living in households scattered across a city, like the Word of God community in Ann Arbor, Michigan, and the John the Baptist Charismatic Renewal community in San Francisco, California, to a small group of ten or a dozen under one roof like a Baptist community in Heywood, Lancashire, and the Barnabas Fellowship at Whatcombe House.

Communities develop either within an existing congregation (for convenience, we will call them "parochial") or outside the normal structures of the denominations ("extra-parochial"). The former are involved with the ministry of the congregation, supplementing it and extending it because of the resources available within the community. These parochial communities have often grown up without much planning—they just happened when members of a prayer group began to spend more time together. In some places they take the form of linked households—two or three families and single individuals sharing a meal and an evening of fellowship together each week and supporting one another in practical ways. One such community I know sets Wednesdays aside as their "fellowship day", refusing to accept any engagement in order to spend time with one another. Other communities are created when a group live together in a large house or rectory. Stephen Davis and his wife of St. Margaret's Church, Durham, have shared their rectory with others like this for some years. One single man is the full-time assistant to the rector. Two others are at work, contributing to the maintenance of the community. A more extensive network of several communities has appeared in other churches like St. Cuthbert's, York.

Extra-parochial communities engage in ministries both within their own walls and beyond in other congregations. The community at Fellowship House, Pilgrim's Hatch, Brentwood, consisting of about a dozen married and single Christians, arranges weekend conferences for groups and study days for ministers from East London and Essex and beyond. Other communities offer the support of a Christian group for those in need of such support for a period of time. The Community of Celebration in its houses at Post Green and elsewhere has ministered to many people in this way.

The distinction between the teaching and the supporting ministry is not clearcut. Most communities, in fact, get involved in both, but with a greater emphasis on one than the other. In the early years at Whatcombe House we were often rung up by clergy, social workers and hospital staff and asked if we could provide a home for a few weeks for some individual who was in need of the support of a Christian fellowship—usually the trouble had been mental and the problem had arisen how to help the sufferer to adjust to more normal living. At first we accepted these people and tried to care for them. Gradually, however, we found that more and more of our time and energy was being sapped by these folk and the work for which we believed God had called us together began to be neglected. Groups of thirty-five people lived with us for weekends and weeks for training and counselling and they required all our attention. The invalids were a distraction to our guests as well as ourselves. The Fellowship spent many months agonising over this problem. It was frequently the subject of prayer meetings and community discussions. In the end, with great reluctance, we decided that we must refuse requests of this kind. We shrank from telling those who rang us up that we couldn't take their cases. We were asked what we thought we were there for, and there were hints that we didn't deserve to be called Christians! But our original vision for Whatcombe House was a place where members of local churches could come and stay with us, sharing in our corporate life and worship to be built up as communities in their own neighbourhood, and by remaining faithful to that vision we were saved from the strain of trying to do too many things at once. It was also a lesson in learning how to be obedient to God rather than to man.

While I was a member of the Barnabas Fellowship we experienced the transition of the community from parochial to extra-parochial character. During the first nine months, while we were preparing Whatcombe House as a conference centre, we were able to go to the village church on Sundays and join in their various activities. But once the house was opened and guests were coming for weeks and weekends, we could no longer do this. All our time was occupied with the community's ministry at Whatcombe. We did not cut ourselves off from the village church completely, but we could not be very deeply involved with them any more. We had become a residential house church with our own Sunday worship and "congregational" activities.*

Community living requires a deep commitment of the members of the community to one another. The average member of a local church can opt out of its life if he wishes to—he can just stay at home and withdraw his support from things that do not attract him. Not all members of congregations do this, of course: some can be very dedicated to the life of their churches. But many have only loose attachments to their congregation. As long as the community member lives with his group, his commitment has to be total. He has a voice in the decision-making process (if the community is properly structured) but, once the decision is made, he is involved in working it out. The community is, in this respect, more like an extended family than a typical congregation. For some Christians, living in what is often a self-centred kind of society, this depth of commitment can be frightening. Single men and women, used to ordering their lives according to their own personal inclinations, realise with a shock that their time is no longer their own. Married couples with children have to adjust to sharing their family circle with others, with all the tensions that

* See my *The Beginnings of Whatcombe: an Experience of Community* (Hodder and Stoughton, 1975).

differing expectations and customs can cause. Without a deep commitment to one another, the community would disintegrate.

Members of a community need a common vision. What has the Lord called us together for? This question should be clearly answered before any practical steps are taken to start a community. A group of Christian friends, influenced by the charismatic renewal, can easily develop a romantic notion that it would be nice to live together. This notion is all the more prevalent because there is nowadays a sort of one-up-man-ship about community living in certain charismatic circles. The suggestion is put about that somehow you are not such a committed Christian if you don't throw your lot in with a community (the old "double standard" which has haunted the Church for centuries appearing once again). As I have just described, it was our common vision of what God's purpose was for the Barnabas Fellowship—confirmed both before and after the establishment of the community by various charismatic manifestations—that enabled us to make important decisions affecting our life together.

A community also needs some form of pooling of resources. Members have to be willing to share what they possess according to their own ability and the needs of others. It is an outward expression of their common life, and it presents a formidable challenge to the materialism of our Western society in which the ambition of so many is a higher salary and better possessions. How this is worked out, again, is a matter in which each community has to seek the Lord's guidance. Flexibility is essential—being willing to try another policy if the first doesn't work. But out of this pooling members receive other blessings: freedom from material concerns that is like an escape from prison; time to spend in doing the things that the Lord requires of us rather than in earning money to meet the next bills; joy in being available for others without the constant anxiety of doing the next domestic chore. A well-organised community provides an environment within which each member discovers new gifts and sees new victories from the Lord.

The relationship between the parochial community and the congregation of which it is a part has to be watched with particular care. Some in the congregation feel challenged by what appears to be the greater commitment of the community members. If the pastor is a member of the community, then others in the congregation may feel that now they cannot be as close to him as when he was an isolated clergyman ministering to all at the same level. The antidote to these fears and suspicions is in the concern of the community for the congregation and the neighbourhood from which it draws its membership. By living as a community, more adults are freed for a full-time ministry; consequently they have time for others in a way that those who go to work (wives as well as husbands) cannot have. It is this deliberate renunciation of the right to independence and the right to salaried employment (about which we hear so much in political discussions these days) that enables a local congregation to enjoy the services of men and women who are as committed to the ministry as the pastor himself.

Most communities are soon surrounded with a host of supporters and wellwishers. Some organise this interest through a newsletter and other links, like the "Friends of Lee Abbey". People can be regarded as community members or associates even though they do not share in the life of the community in the same way as those who are all under one roof. Such a network of relationships can be built up within a local church round one or more of the communities within it, although it is likely that in time the network will spread beyond the immediate membership of that local church as that community's ministry spreads. The traditional religious orders of the Roman Catholic and Anglican Churches have never been limited to particular parishes, and it looks as if the modern communities are outgrowing their parent congregations in the same way. Nevertheless there is considerable advantage to both the community and the congregation if the links between them remain strong. The community can help the congregation to realise in its life and worship what fellowship in the Holy Spirit can be; the congregation can assist the community to relate in a realistic manner to the neighbourhood of which it is a part.

Although no charismatic community can be described as typical, the Christian Renewal Centre at Rostrevor in Northern Ireland is an example of how the lessons of Pentecostalism aided a group of Christians to come together in a way that has political and social significance in a troubled land. Cecil Kerr, the Church of Ireland chaplain in the Queen's University, Belfast, and his wife, Myrtle, were baptised in the Holy Spirit in 1971. I described in a previous chapter one of the weekends organised by Cecil. Early in 1973 God spoke to them and other members of their prayer group concerning what he was going to do in Ireland. Through visions and prophecies he showed them an army of people marching through the country with the cross of Christ at the head, lifeless bodies rising up along the way to join the procession of praise. God told them he wanted to light fires of love in every part of the land. Their task was to establish a place where Christians from all traditions could come together in a spirit of love and prayer. After much discussion and waiting on God, they decided to launch out in faith.

The problem of finance loomed up immediately. After various suggestions, a young economics graduate said, "I believe that God wants you to do this. He will put it into the hearts of the right people to give the right amount at the right time." "It was," commented Cecil, "a financial principle that the young man hadn't discovered in his economics textbooks!" A simple brochure was sent out to friends, and the money began to come in. A house in Rostrevor was purchased. Situated on the east coast of Ireland, it stands on the border between Northern Ireland and the Republic of Ireland. It is ideally situated as a place of reconciliation: the two parts of the beautiful but divided country are clearly visible from the house's windows.

The community was established in 1975 and its members represent the Anglican, Roman Catholic, Presbyterian and Methodist traditions. It is living evidence that Christian unity is possible across the divisions that exist in Ireland. Members commit themselves for a year or more. No one receives a salary, and any money earned outside the community goes towards the work of the Centre. The community meets for prayer morning and evening but on Sundays attends churches in Rostrevor.

On Monday evenings about eighty people come for two hours of praise and prayer. Many return for another evening for Bible study or *Growth in the Spirit* seminars. About one hundred gather on Tuesday evenings for a prayer meeting at a hotel nearby once bombed by the I.R.A. Not long ago a British army patrol called to investigate. The soldiers were astonished to discover Roman Catholics and Protestants meeting peacefully together to worship Almighty God! Days of renewal are organised. Clergy and congregations from Belfast and elsewhere visit the Centre for days or weekends. People physically and emotionally broken by the violence and hatred of the past years have been wonderfully healed and renewed. With a team Cecil is frequently invited to talk about charismatic renewal and introduce groups to ministry in the Holy Spirit in different parts of Ireland. His message is that there is a love released at the cross of Christ which destroys every barrier that Satan erects. In a thousand simple yet profound ways God works in the hearts of those who meet the community to break down the walls of fear and hatred.

The story of Rostrevor illustrates the particular witness of community life. It focusses attention on the fellowship of Christians—what it means to be committed to one another in Jesus Christ. In Belfast and in other parts of Northern Ireland there have been various attempts to show that Roman Catholics and Protestants are one in the Lord. There have been united carol services at Christmas and united acts of worship on Good Friday. There are many ecumenical prayer groups both north and south of the Border. Impressive though these signs of unity are, they do not carry the message of reconciliation so powerfully as the community where Roman Catholics and Protestants *live* together under one roof, demonstrating the love of Jesus Christ by sharing together their possessions, their worship and their work. By its very existence such a community speaks of mutual forgiveness and acceptance more loudly than all the speeches of politicians and the sermons of clerics.

For a community has to be a place where forgiveness is known if it is to exist. I remember one occasion at Whatcombe House when the members of the community—without any visitors in the house on that day, as it happened—assembled in the little chapel one morning for a Communion service feeling disheartened and disgruntled with one another. At the end of a busy season of conferences individual members had been hurt unintentionally by others in the community and there was much misunderstanding in the air. Reg East led the eucharist in the usual way. A reading from the Bible, a discussion and some intercessions. When we came to the general confession, a member of the Fellowship burst out: "It's no good, Reg. I can't go on with this. I don't feel we're in a fit state to receive Communion together." After a shocked pause, the rest of us agreed with him.

Reg then did a wise thing. He suggested that we left the chapel and went about our work for the rest of the morning. After lunch he said, we could have a special community meeting to talk the matter through. This we did. By the time we met in the afternoon we were more prepared to face one another openly. Two hours were spent in reviewing the situation. Each member was able to say what he or she felt. Apologies were given and misunderstandings were cleared up. At about four o'clock we went back into the chapel—the books were still open in the places where we had left them and the bread and the wine were still in the vessels on the altar-table. We said the general confession together and Reg pronounced the absolution. We felt cleansed by God because we had experienced forgiveness from one another. We embraced each other in the Peace and received the sacrament with tremendous thanksgiving. I do not think I have ever experienced an act of worship in which the joy of repentance overwhelmed the proceedings with such thanksgiving.

Some have detected in these charismatic communities and other groupings the beginnings of an alternative society. They have suggested that in an age when the individual counts for little in society and when the nuclear family is being destroyed by the pressures of modern life, men and women are exploring new forms of association which recreate the basic communities of yesterday—the extended family, the closely-knit village, the manor with its dependants, the neighbourhood of the pre-war street in East London. Coupled with this is the increasing realisation that the life-style of Western man will have to be simplified if the resources of the world are to be distributed more equally—and it is a fact of experience that ten people in a community can live more cheaply than five couples in their own homes. Furthermore, community life of one kind or another has always been a feature of the Church—the religious orders are the descendants of those who were drawn to a closer form of community life as a result of renewal movements in previous centuries.

Whether they are the beginnings of an alternative society or not, charismatic communities are certainly prophetic signs to the local churches. Through them the Lord is asking his people to examine what it means to relate to one another in Jesus Christ through the Holy Spirit. The communities are saying to us something like this: "Commitment to Jesus Christ means commitment to one another. For us, this commitment means living together in a form that enables each of us to be released into a fuller ministry by the Holy Spirit. The difficulties we encounter are means of growing into Jesus Christ; the joys we share are a foretaste of the life of heaven. What does commitment to one another mean in terms of your lifestyle?"

It is likely that the members of communities will always remain a small minority within the total membership of the denominations. I cannot see large numbers of Christian families deserting their semi-detached homes and going to live in big houses in the cities or the countryside. But I can see more of them seeking a deeper fellowship with other members of their congregation in ways that affect their lifestyle. The charismatic prayer group and the house church have already emerged as examples of this.

The lesson from these developments is, I believe, that we should not be too quick to draw a distinction between a congregation, a house church and a community. Basically they are each gatherings of Christians who have been brought together by the Holy Spirit to worship and serve the Father through their union in his Son. The differences are to be found in the manner of their response to God's call: the congregation responds within the traditional structures, the house church in new-found relationships of a more informal kind, and the community in a deeper degree of commitment to one another. But between the congregation with its prayer groups, the house church and its links with the local churches in its neighbourhood, and the communities which are parochial or extra-parochial, the line of demarcation is often blurred. I suspect that it is we who create the differences rather than the Lord.

16

Charismatic and Institutional

In this final chapter we ought to glance at some of the implications of renewal for the wider fellowship of which the local church is just a small part. For no congregation exists in isolation from others. Even the most independent local church has some sort of a network through which it relates to others (and on which it is often a good deal more dependent than most of its members realise). Michael Harper has called the ministry of this wider fellowship "translocal". This is a useful term, for it can be applied to the ministry of all those who exercise an oversight of the congregations in their denominations, from bishops and their diocesan officials to the Methodist Conference and the chairmen of districts. When a local church is touched by the renewing power of the Holy Spirit, those exercising this translocal ministry begin to feel the effects, just as the strings of a harp higher up the scale begin to vibrate when the strings lower down are plucked.

The translocal structure of a denomination's ministry is almost inevitably associated with the institutional dimension of the Church in people's minds. The machinery for overseeing the congregations, which includes the consultative and decision-making processes of synods and councils and the permanent committees and boards with their officers, seems to embody everything that has to do with permanency and legality. Nothing, it would appear, could be less charismatic. Indeed, many of those who staff this machinery seem to be hostile to change and spontaneity. Perhaps behind their reaction is a hint of fear that their status is being threatened and their authority questioned by charismatic movements within the local churches. Hence the idea goes round that the charismatic and the institutional are opposed to one another. But the fact is, of course, that when we talk about the institutional, we are talking about *people*. Although the traditional structures have a form of their own, they could not operate unless they were staffed by our fellow Christian men and women. And these men and women are themselves called to be open to the Holy Spirit, and they are also members of congregations.

If the ministry of such Christians—from bishops downwards—is to be fruitful, it must also be charismatic. "Helpers" and "administrators" are listed alongside "healers" and "speakers in various kinds of tongues" in I Corinthians 12.28. (*Antilēpsis* was a technical term in the field of banking and referred to the work of an accountant; we have already noted that *kybernēsis* stemmed from the language of sailors and denoted the man at the helm: from this it came to mean leading or managing a business.) They, too, then need the fresh anointing of the Holy Spirit that the translocal ministry of the Church may be renewed. Consequently those involved in the institutional dimension of the Church need those involved in the charismatic dimension, and vice versa. Without the charismatic, the institutional becomes hard and rigid and survives only as long as people are prepared to bow down to it. The charismatic without the institutional bursts like a bubble, exhausting itself to proclaim its message and failing to fulfil its proper function within the Church.

If the charismatic renewal is going to bring new life to the local churches, the translocal ministry must be able to hear what God is saying through the movement to the Church, and especially to their denomination, and make appropriate responses in obedience to him. It is extremely important, therefore, that good lines of communication should be established between those leading the charismatic renewal in the local churches and those whose ministry lies within the translocal structures. A breakdown here could rob the wider Church of the blessings God is bestowing on his people locally.

To illustrate this I would like to describe the steps taken by charismatic Roman Catholics in the United States to keep their hierarchy informed of the renewal in their denomination and the effect this has had on the attitude of their church leaders. The story of the beginnings of the charismatic renewal among American Roman Catholics is fairly wellknown. It was first experienced among them in Duquesne University in Pittsburgh in 1967 and spread rapidly. Within two years the Committee on Doctrine had been asked to submit a report on the renewal to the Roman

Catholic bishops of the United States at their national conference in Washington. The speed with which this report was prepared and presented is remarkable. Admittedly by the period 1967–69 Roman Catholic charismatics had the benefit of drawing on the experiences of charismatics in other denominations, especially the Episcopalians. Nevertheless it is noteworthy that several competent Roman Catholic theologians had become personally involved in the movement and that they took steps to inform their hierarchy what was happening and to suggest guidelines for them.

The report was fairly brief. After noting the spread of the renewal in the previous two years, it warned that "judgments are often based on superficial knowledge" and suggested that "more scholarly research is needed". It pointed out that "theologically the movement has legitimate basis for existence" and that "the most prudent way to judge the validity of the claims of the movement is to observe the effects on those who participate in the prayer meetings". In the final paragraph the report said: "It is the conclusion of the Committee on Doctrine that the movement should at this point not be inhibited but allowed to develop. Certain cautions, however, must be exercised. Proper supervision can be effectively exercised only if the bishops keep in mind their pastoral responsibility to oversee and guide this movement in the Church. We must be on guard that it avoids the mistakes of classic Pentecostalism. It must be recognised that in our culture there is a tendency to substitute religious experience for religious doctrine. In practice, we recommend that bishops involve prudent priests to be associated with this movement. Such involvement and guidance would be welcomed by the Catholic Pentecostals."*

In 1970 the National Service Committee of the Catholic Charismatic Renewal of the United States was set up, composed of a number of laity and clergy (including one bishop) who were regarded as leaders of the movement in various parts of the country. This committee set up other groups, including an International Communication Office, which moved to Brussels in 1976.

The National Service Committee defined its responsibilities as being:

* The report is printed as an appendix in *The Pentecostal Movement in the Catholic Church* by Edward D. O'Connor (Ave Maria Press, Indiana, 1971) pp. 291–3, and its preparation is described on pp. 19–21.

pastoral supervision of the national conferences of the Catholic charismatic renewal in the United States, and appropriate participation in the pastoral supervision of the international conferences;

pastoral planning in conjunction with regional leaders of the regional general conferences of the Catholic charismatic renewal in the United States;

communication with the National Conference of Catholic Bishops in the United States, and the promotion of communication with their hierarchy worldwide through the International Communication Office in Brussels;

sponsoring of a variety of conferences, workshops and forums on vital issues, such as the roles of men and women in the charismatic renewal, approaches to ecumenism within the charismatic renewal, and theological reflection on the charismatic renewal;

shaping the editorial policy of the *New Covenant* magazine;

promotion of communication throughout the charismatic renewal through newsletters;

promotion of communication with and among prayer group leaders and local and regional committees and service teams;

assembling and publishing of a prayer group directory;

coordination and communication with the religious and secular press through a press department;

providing of assistance in contacting and obtaining speakers for various events;

funding and distribution of literature to those in need in the United States and overseas;

fund-raising activities on behalf of leaders of the charismatic renewal in poorer countries of the world to enable them to travel to and participate in leaders' meetings and training sessions.

"The National Service Committee is committed to continued service of the Church through its pastoral concern and service to the Catholic charismatic renewal," it said. "We feel increasingly that the Lord is giving us a maturity of insight into the conditions and problems confronting the renewal, the Church and the world in the present day. It is our intention, in collaboration with the hierarchy and other leaders of the renewal, to pursue the growth, maturation, content and direction of the charismatic renewal in the Catholic Church and in the whole of Christianity."*

A key figure in this story is Cardinal Leon-Joseph Suenens, Archbishop of Malines-Brussels and Primate of the Roman Catholic Church in Belgium. At the Second Vatican Council the Cardinal made a speech on the charismatic nature of the Church, and he has involved himself in the charismatic renewal since its first beginnings in his own denomination. He describes his experiences in *A New Pentecost?* † including his own personal renewal in the Spirit. No doubt much of his wisdom is responsible for the careful policies of the American Roman Catholic charismatic leaders.

The charismatic renewal now became the subject for consultation on a world basis. An international group of theologians and charismatic leaders (some from Pentecostal and other Protestant Churches) began to meet each year from 1972 onwards to discuss a number of related topics—Pentecostal spirituality, the role of personal experience in the Christian faith, charismatic movements in the history of the Church, charisms and sacraments, the discerning of spirits, and so on. The group reported after the first five years and identified other areas deserving further study. The particular value of this group is that by encouraging competent theologians to keep up a process of continual assessment of the charismatic renewal (some of them being personally helped very much by it in the process), the translocal ministry of the Roman Catholic Church is being presented with material that assists the hierarchy in discerning the way the Holy Spirit is leading their congregations under the impetus of this movement.‡

* *New Covenant*, December 1977 (Volume 7, No. 6) p. 33.

† First edition in French, 1974; English translation published by Darton, Longman and Todd in 1975.

‡ The papers and report of this Pentecostal-Catholic dialogue (as it is called) are printed in the following numbers of the magazine *One in Christ* (Benedictine Convent, Priory Close, London N14 4AT): vol. ix, no. 1 (1973); vol. x, no. 2 (1974); vol. xii, no. 4 (1976), and vol. xiii, no. 1 (1977).

In 1974 lay leaders in the renewal and six theologians met with Cardinal Suenens to prepare the document from which I quoted earlier in this book, *Theologican and Pastoral Orientations on the Catholic Charismatic Renewal*. The document sets the renewal movement within the context of the Church's continuing life and examines its theologican basis. It also points to matters concerned with evaluating the movement and relating it to the pastoral situations in which Roman Catholics find themselves throughout the world. At the end the authors repeat the request made by Pope John at the Second Vatican Council: "Be open to what the Spirit is saying to the Churches!" The document was distributed to all the bishops attending the synod on evangelism in Rome in that year—the synod which prompted the Pope to write his apostolic exhortation, quoted in an earlier chapter. The following year an international charismatic conference was held in Rome during the Whitsun weekend, culminating in a mass in St. Peter's during which prophecies were spoken, ten thousand participants sang in the Spirit, and Pope Paul embraced Cardinal Suenens.

To the charismatics the Pope said: "Reflect on the two names by which you are designated, 'Spirit-ual Renewal'. Where the Spirit is concerned we are immediately alert (the Pope was referring to himself in a 'royal we'). More than that, we invite him, we pray to him, we desire nothing more than that Christians, believing people, should experience an awareness, a worship, a greater joy through the Holy Spirit of God among us. Have we forgotten the Holy Spirit? Certainly not! We want him, we honour him, we love him, and we invoke him. And you, with your devotion and fervour, wish to live in the Spirit. This should be where your second name comes in—Renewal. It ought to rejuvenate the world, give it back a spirituality, a soul, and religious thought. It ought to open its closed lips to prayer and to song, to joy, to hymns, and to witnessing. It will be very fortuitous for our times, for our brothers, that there should be a generation, your generation of young people, who shout out to the world the glory and the greatness of the God of Pentecost . . ."

To the other worshippers in St. Peter's the Pope added: "The second message is for those pilgrims present at this great assembly who do not belong to your movement. They should unite themselves with you to celebrate the feast of Pentecost—the spiritual renewal of the world, of our society, and of our souls—so that they too, devout pilgrims to this centre of the Catholic faith, might nourish themselves on the enthusiasm and the spiritual energy with which we must live our religion. And we will say only this: today, either one lives one's faith with devotion, depth, energy and joy, or that faith will die out."*

This, then, is how the leaders of the charismatic renewal in the Roman Catholic Church are attempting to help their hierarchy appreciate what is happening among them. No doubt to the European reader it all sounds rather like a successful American business company going international and flinging its tendrons round the world! But at least the American Roman Catholic charismatics have taken the universal nature of their denomination seriously (and have at the same time offered their help to many in other denominations as well). The result is that the charismatic renewal is now recognised officially within the trans-local structures of that denomination and has been commended by the Pope himself. Consequently a Roman Catholic bishop, priest or layman can identify himself with the renewal without feeling that he should be apologetic about it.

The charismatic renewal still has much to teach this oldest denomination in the Western world. Prayer meetings in Roman Catholic parishes still remain only prayer meetings without much impact on the parish itself. The numerous communities that have sprung up in the United States have had very little effect on the parochial structures. And I doubt whether many Roman Catholic bishops and priests have yet begun to realise what an every-member ministry can mean in a highly clericalised denomination! Nevertheless, the lines of communication have been laid for the charismatic and the institutional dimensions of that Church to assist one another. The policy of the National Service Committee in the United States has been copied elsewhere. The bishops of the Roman Catholic Church in England and Wales have appointed one of their number, Bishop Langton Fox of Menevia (a diocese in Wales) as their "ecclesiastical assistant" to the National Service Committee in this country. Bishop Fox has involved himself in the charismatic renewal—attending prayer meetings, meeting charismatics in other denominations, and leading his own prayer group—and he reports back to his fellow bishops.

Those responsible for translocal ministries in other denomi-

* *Text in New Covenant*, July 1975 (Volume 5, No. 1) pp. 23–5.

nations could profitably think and pray about these developments in the Roman Catholic Church. They illustrate one way in which an international Christian community, generally regarded as one of the most traditional and rigid among ecclesiastical structures, is bringing together its institutional and charismatic elements. Shouldn't leaders in other Christian communities be doing the same thing? Is it enough just to have a ninety minutes' debate in a Methodist synod or a diocesan conference on the charismatic movement? Isn't it necessary to have something like a service committee within each denomination to provide links between national structures and those in the forefront of the movement in the local churches? Ecumenical bodies like the Fountain Trust in England can do invaluable work in teaching about renewal in those many aspects that affect all Christians, but each denomination needs help in discerning how to test and apply the lessons of the movement to its own traditions and needs. Such service committees might well be closely associated with existing boards for mission and lay training in the denominations. Personally I would prefer to keep the adjective "charismatic" out of the title of any new structure: something like "Renewal and Congregational Life" would be better.

The story of the charismatic renewal in the Roman Catholic Church also indicates how useful it is to involve doctrinal commissions and other theological groups in what is happening. One of the strengths of the renewal among Roman Catholics is that from the early days its participants called in wellknown theologians and fearlessly exposed their experiences to the questions and advice of scholars. Since many of the first Roman Catholic charismatics were on the staffs of universities and seminaries, it was perhaps natural that they should do this, but it demonstrated a willingness to test the Pentecostal gifts of the Spirit with those other gifts that God has given the theologians. And, when all is said and done, the true ministry of theology is to contemplate the will and ways of God!

Contrast the story of the Roman Catholic charismatics with the shorter stories of two friends of mine. One, an Anglican priest, was baptised in the Holy Spirit and dutifully wrote to his diocesan bishop to share the good news. He received a chilly letter in reply. It was obvious that the bishop had no idea what my friend was talking about and had assumed that he was suffering from some sort of religious delusion. He didn't exactly tell him to go and see a doctor, but it was that kind of a reply! The result was a complete loss of trust in one another. A wiser bishop would have taken more care to find out more about my friend's experiences—and for this, the kind of service committee that I have suggested would have been useful. The other friend was an Anglican layman who came into a leadership role in the charismatic movement locally. He was invited to preside regularly over a growing prayer meeting that drew its participants from a wide area. His vicar was alarmed by this. He assumed that my friend was trying to build up a rival congregation and ordered him not to go to the meetings any more. My friend endeavoured to explain the situation to the vicar, but without success. Eventually my friend ceased to attend his parish church and joined a house church where in a few years he became an elder. Again, if there had been advisers on the charismatic renewal within the Church of England—perhaps within each diocese—the story might have ended happily. As it is, the Church of England has lost a member with outstanding charisms of pastoral leadership.

Of course, we cannot hope to organise the wind of renewal through the denominational structures any more than we can hope to organise it in the local church. The hither-and-thither movement of the Holy Spirit sweeps through all our carefully planned arrangements. "In the pentecostal movement," wrote Dr. Donald Coggan, the Archbishop of Canterbury, recently, "God is at work in his Church—disturbingly at work, perhaps, in our regimented minds, untidily at work—but then wind and fire are untidy, unpredictable elements, and these are the metaphors in which scripture speaks of the Spirit." Yet the Spirit is also a God of order, and when he manifests himself through individuals and groups in the Church, we can expect him to do this in a way which has a continuity with the past—with those institutions and traditions which were instituted and handed down through his inspiration. For the ecclesiastical institutions renewal means adapting rather than abolishing. The history of the Church teaches us that she has always been most successful when she has been able to adapt herself to the new forms of congregation and ministry that God has raised up at different times and in different places.

In this connection, two matters require immediate attention. The first concerns the way in which many Christians are coming together in fellowship in contemporary society; the second concerns the charismatic leaders of groups and ordination. We have already talked round these topics and they need only brief mention as illustrations of how the institutional could adapt itself to the charismatic in the Church now.

We have seen how, as the Spirit renews the people of God, the concept of belonging to the Church has much greater meaning for many in the small group situation rather than in the traditional congregation. And we have also seen that in this cellular pattern of the local church the every-member ministry is more likely to be realised. This lesson has been emerging for a long time. It was presented in 1945 in the Church of England report *Towards the Conversion of England*; it has been reiterated many times since in books and documents down to such publications as *A Time for Building*, a report prepared by a Roman Catholic working party in England on pastoral strategy in 1976, and the material prepared for the second National Evangelical Anglican Congress in 1977, *Obeying Christ in a Changing World.** The charismatic movement has underlined this lesson with the added truth that any Christian group can only serve Jesus Christ if all its members are willing to be open to the Holy Spirit personally. To say that within and outside the traditional congregations there is growing up another network of groups, which are in some instances becoming little churches—"churches of the little flock", as Karl Rahner has aptly christened them†—is not to say anything very revolutionary. It has been happening for more than a quarter of a century—at least.

Yet in their policies the translocal ministries of the denominations have hardly given any sign that they have noticed the emergence of these important new basic Christian communities. Administration is still geared to the maintenance of the present pastoral pattern. Clergy are still being trained on the assumption that they will one day be in sole charge of a congregation gathered in a building, and that they will be expected to engage in all sorts

---

* *Towards the Conversion of England* (Press and Publications Board of the Church Assembly, 1945), pp. 70ff.; *A Time for Building* (Catholic Information Services, 1976), pp. 28–9; *Obeying Christ in a Changing World*, vol. 2, ed. Ian Cundy (Collins, 1977) pp. 46ff.

† Karl Rahner, *The Shape of the Church to Come* (SPCK, 1972) pp. 108ff.

of diverse activities in order to minister to that congregation (the
assumption that there will always be "a sacred place, a holy man,
and a sinful people", as I once heard it described). Only rarely is
there news of a translocal ministry that is spending more money
on lay training than on clergy training, or that is initiating a bold
ecumenical project in which traditional, denominational structures are being ignored and an opportunity is being taken to
encourage the growth of a local church in a new form. This is one
area in which greater discernment and more adaptation is necessary.

The second is closely related to it. As the groups multiply and
become established as basic Christian communities, shouldn't the
Church recognise this work of the Spirit and unite the more
permanent of these groups to the wider fellowship by ordaining
their leaders? If so, this would mean a revision of the way in which
the denominations select and train men and women for the
ordained ministry today. I do not wish to sound as if I am
condemning willy-nilly the present system, whereby students are
sent to a theological college or a seminary and then appointed to
local churches at the end of their course when they are ordained.
The Church will always need theologically equipped men and
women, who can be sent on apostolic ministries into local
churches for special purposes and go out as evangelistic teams to
open up new work. What I am saying is that there does seem
something fundamentally wrong with a policy which permits *only*
those who have undertaken an academic course to be ordained.

A development along these lines raises other questions about
ordination, especially among Anglicans and Roman Catholics.
How would it affect our theology of ordination? What is the right
relationship between spiritual gift and sacramental sign? What
problems of discipline would it raise, within denominations as
well as across their boundaries? Can we maintain a doctrine of the
indelibility of orders and still ordain an individual to a presidency
in a church of the little flock that might vanish in a couple of
years? What would be the effects on the full-time clergy? There is
certainly much to talk about (though the debate has been going on
already for quite a long time!). But I am convinced that these
questions are very secondary compared with the need for translocal ministries to encourage and support the many new groups
that we find everywhere in the local church today by ordaining,

where it would be appropriate, those whom the Holy Spirit has gifted with pastoral leadership among their members.

It is a matter of adapting an older policy to the new circumstances. Up until recently the local churches multiplied through a process of growth in geographical areas. When the population of a Church of England parish increased, the process began with the building of a "mission church"—usually a temporary construction—in that part of the parish where the new houses were going up. If successful, the "mission church" was replaced by a "daughter church" which was a more substantial construction. By this time, too, a curate from the staff of the parish was assigned to the daughter church and given special charge for it. Finally, if the congregation was able to support itself without help from the "mother church", the geographical area became a separate parish and the building was designated a parish church. But, as we have seen, these conditions, dependent upon a congregation from a geographical area becoming large enough to maintain a church building and a full-time pastor, no longer apply in many areas of modern society. Church growth is taking place in other groupings—groupings that do not depend so much on permanent church buildings and full-time pastors. To ordain suitable leaders in the churches of the little flock without withdrawing them for unnecessary training and without expecting them to exercise a full-time ministry, is only adjusting the older policy to the new opportunities.

The encouraging thing about this second matter is that there are indications that it is already beginning to happen. The Roman Catholic Church has revised the diaconate in order to ordain leaders among the laity to positions of pastoral responsibility in the denomination. The deacon does not have the same ministry as the priest (who is fulfilling a function of presidential leadership in a congregation), but the two are not so far apart that they could not draw closer together. In the Free Churches, officials such as elders and deacons and lay preachers are assuming greater responsibility for pastoral leadership in local churches as the numbers of full-time ordained men and women decline. And the Anglican Church—in England and elsewhere—has set up schemes whereby men (and women in some provinces) can be trained for ordination whilst they are still in secular employment and continue in their jobs after ordination. Furthermore, in some

Church of England parishes where an eldership has been established, the diocesan bishop has been invited to commission new elders in a service which includes prayer with the laying on of hands.

Much more could be said about these things, but we must draw our discussion to a close. We began with baptism in the Holy Spirit as a personal experience of God's love and the effect this has on an individual Christian in his congregation. We have ended with an attempt to show how the charismatic dimension in the Church can be related to the institutional. But at the heart of it is the conviction that God is pouring out his Spirit on all flesh in these days and renewing his people as the living body of Jesus Christ. The signs of this renewal are in many places. Some of them we call the charismatic movement. But the time will come, perhaps fairly soon, when we shall not have to distinguish the charismatic renewal in that way, for by then the movement will have fulfilled its purpose. It will have lost itself in that older and greater charismatic movement which is the Spirit-filled Church of Jesus Christ. It will have disappeared as a river disappears when its waters reach the estuary and mingle with those of the one and only sea.

Then the Church—in congregations, groups, house churches and communities—will be pulsating with the life of God, subject to his Word, anointed by his Spirit, constrained by his love, preaching his Good News, and ministering with his power.

> Behold, I am doing a new thing;
> now it springs forth, do you not perceive it?
> I will make a way in the wilderness
> and rivers in the desert.
> The wild beasts will honour me,
> the jackals and the ostriches;
> for I give water in the wilderness,
> rivers in the desert,
> to give drink to my chosen people,
> the people whom I formed for myself
> that they might declare my praise.
> (Isaiah 43.19–21)